GUSTAVE EIFFEL

Henri Loyrette

GUSTAVE EIFFEL

RIZZOLI
NEW YORK

Translation from the French by
Rachel and Susan Gomme; architectural and stylistic adviser, Andor Gomme

French-language edition, *Eiffel – Un ingénieur et son œuvre*
Copyright © 1985 by Office du Livre S.A.
Fribourg, Switzerland

English translation:
Copyright © 1985 by Office du Livre S.A.,
Fribourg, Switzerland

English translation published in 1985 in the
United States of America by:

*R*IZZOLI *INTERNATIONAL PUBLICATIONS, INC.*
597 Fifth Avenue/New York 10017

Library of Congress Cataloging in Publication Data

Loyrette, Henri.
    Gustave Eiffel.

    Bibliography: p.
    Includes index.
    1. Eiffel, Gustave, 1832–1923.   2. Tour Eiffel
(Paris, France)   3. Engineers—France—Biography.
I. Title.
TA140.E4L6913   1985   624'.092'4 [B]   85-42913
ISBN 0-8478-0631-6

Printed and bound in Switzerland

Contents

Introduction

The curious album of Dufrénoy, *Dans l'intimité de personnages illustres,* contains two photographs relating to Gustave Eiffel. One, dating from 1882, is an all-too-rare portrait of Eiffel as an easy-going family man, surrounded by four of his five children. The other seems incongruous in a series which otherwise consists only of portraits. It shows the Eiffel Tower in 1888, when it had been built only as far as the second platform. Underneath is a caption in childish writing, which reads: "To surprise Daddy, I am sticking in this album the photo of the Eiffel Tower [which will] be 300 meters high...," thus referring to that aspect of the monument that made it stand out. The father conscientiously corrects his son's inapposite comment: "My little boy has confused great men with great monuments."[1]

In Eiffel's case it is not only little boys who confuse great men with great monuments; indeed the tower, whether seen as a masterpiece or as showing a "total insensitivity to art"[2] conceals not only the man but his whole career. Eiffel *is* the tower. The best-informed may add to it some noteworthy works of engineering in France and Portugal but know nothing of the rest of his achievements, of the difficulties of his early career, his childhood in Dijon, his studies in Paris, the building of the bridge at Bordeaux, or the risks entailed in his first commissions.

The fault lies not so much with Eiffel himself, who, when late in life he wrote his *Biographie industrielle et scientifique* (1923),[3] neglected no single phase of his long career, as with the image we have of him, which is the one he assuredly wanted to leave to posterity. Eiffel is the engineer, the "great man" as the nineteenth century conceived him and supplied the model. In that, although still so modern today, he is curiously old-fashioned. And nothing seems likely to correct this image: neither the photographs of the luxurious and imposing homes he lived in after he made his fortune—the town house in the Rue Rabelais in Paris, the Château des Bruyères et Sèvres, the Villa Claire at Vevey, or the Villa Salles at Beaulieu—nor, above all, those of Eiffel himself, always in a stiff pose, conscious of the camera, as if the slightest portrait must have official status. And how should it not, since in his own time, after the triumphant success of the 300-meter tower, his image was everywhere? Paintings of Eiffel, sculptures of Eiffel, Eiffel medallions or medals, Eiffel caricatures, Eiffel knickknacks, Eiffel in the press: all these emblems carefully collected and preserved by his own efforts and those of his daughter Claire. But also Eiffel after his death, the lock of gray hair sealed in an envelope, the will, the settlement of his estate, the interminable list of condolences, and, finally, posterity further magnifying the glory which he knew in his lifetime: public monuments, streetnames, postage stamps, dictionaries, and textbooks.

Valuable information is contributed by sources recently made available to the public: the archives of the Société Levallois-Perret, divided between the Archives Nationales and the Société Nouvelle d'Exploitation de la Tour Eiffel, and above all the Eiffel collection generously given by his descendants to the Musée d'Orsay, which consists essentially of biographical material (correspondence, collections of bills, student drawings, souvenirs, and more relaxed family photographs, right down to place cards and celebration programs—Eiffel's birthday, December 15, was always lavishly celebrated), enable one to correct the impression of a too exemplary life, to animate the overrigid picture.

Eiffel (en 1882)

Le premier ingénieur de France; a jeté des ponts dans le monde entier. Proposait à Panama un gigantesque canal à écluses. On a préféré un canal sans écluses. On a peut-être eu tort. Médite, dit-on, de rebâtir la Tour de Babel dans Paris? Le canal eut été plus utile.

1 *Eiffel in 1882*, photograph published in J.M. Dufrénoy's album *Dans l'intimité de personnages illustres 1850–1900*.

Photo de la Tour
au 2ème étage

pour faire une surprise à papa
moi je colle dans cet albome là
fotografie de la Tour Éfel
caura 300 mètres ou papa ma
promis de me faire monter pendant
lexposicion

Mon petit garçon a confondu les
grands hommes avec les grands monuments.

2 "*Photo of the Tower at the second stage*," photograph published in J.M. Dufrénoy's album *Dans l'intimité de personnages illustres 1850–1900.*

11

3   House inhabited by Gustave Eiffel, 1 Rue Rabelais, Paris, formerly the Jacquemart-André House (demolished).

4   Salon of the Rue Rabelais house.   5   Hall of the Rue Rabelais house. ▷

Though always a figure in the public eye, Eiffel has not attracted much attention from architectural historians; apart from some well-informed remarks of Le Corbusier, he has, curiously enough, been kept in the background by those who have concentrated, somewhat tediously, on the sources of twentieth-century architecture and have seen in every metal construction a forerunner of the daring forms of the future. But today, when a whole forgotten and despised aspect of the nineteenth century, that of Charles Garnier and of Paul Baudry, is being brought to life again, Eiffel also is being rediscovered. Numerous exhibitions and publications—starting with the excellent monographs by Bernard Marrey and Bertrand Lemoine—are evidence of this trend.

After the appearance in 1939 of François Poncetton's fine book (overadulatory though it is and stressing the life at the expense of the work), there was a striking lack of important publications. It took the pioneering enthusiasm of Gilbert Cordier to bring to light, through his frequently pertinent "reflections on the circumstances and methods of nineteenth-century metal construction," a whole series of facts which had been largely forgotten.

Gustave Eiffel, his life and work? Any such title would be hard to live up to, for his work swallows up so much of his private life, from his association with Charles Nepveu to his work on wind resistance in his old age. Moreover, it is impossible to say that the man figures complete in his work, as might be said of a painter or a writer; for each of

◁ 6 *Gustave Eiffel*, photograph c. 1890, Paris, Musée d'Orsay, Eiffel collection.

7 Villa Salles at Beaulieu-sur-Mer.

16

◁ 8 Sketch for a plaque with the head of Gustave Eiffel on a mosaic background, watercolor, Paris, Musée d'Orsay, Eiffel collection.

his works is a cooperative effort. Even if Eiffel contracted for it, he was helped by associates who made drawings and calculations and sometimes, as in the case of the 300-meter tower, took the initiative. So it would be dangerous to talk of Eiffel's style, as one speaks of Garnier's style or Guimard's; but from his first great work, the bridge over the Douro, to the tower itself there is always the same elegance, power, tension, the unmistakable monumentality. Eiffel—as has been said of the tower—came at the right moment and reaped what others had sown, giving to iron construction its last and greatest masterpieces. In that respect he also was a whole epoch: he summed it up and immortalized it.

9   Gustave Eiffel, *Caricature of Madame Mitchine*, "mother and pianist, during a dance organized by her daughter," pen and watercolor, drawn at Nice between 1905 and 1915, Paris, Musée d'Orsay, Eiffel collection.

From Dijon to Levallois:
Childhood, Youth and Early Works

The Eiffel Family

Gustave Eiffel evinced the highest degree of family loyalty. At the end of his life, when writing (in the third person) his *Biographie industrielle et scientifique*, he devoted the first of the four typewritten volumes, *Généalogie de la famille Eiffel*, entirely to his ancestry, relations, and family connections. In it he proliferates pious injunctions, asking his children and grandchildren to revere, as he himself did, the memory of those who had helped, loved, or supported him in difficult times, whether his sister, Madame Hénoque, whose "help had been so valuable to him in the education of his children and in the care devoted to their moral and physical development,"[1] or ancestors whom the children could not have known, such as the Lachapelles, who had left an almost legendary memory. Throughout his life Eiffel demonstrated his concern for and pride in his name, supporting members of his family who were in difficulties, absorbed in settling marriages or inheritances to the best advantage, and himself giving touching demonstrations of filial piety. The difficult marriage negotiations in which he himself engaged in Bordeaux at the beginning of the 1860s, the refusals which he met with and which (as we sense through his correspondence) humiliated him in spite of the jaunty attitude he adopted, his implication in the Panama affair and the subsequent scandal were, in varying degrees, tests for himself and his family and for the name he bore.

The Eiffel family came from Germany, specifically Marmagen, near Cologne. At the very beginning of the eighteenth century, for reasons unknown to us, Jean-René Boenickhausen settled in Paris under the name of Eiffel, which was easier to pronounce than his long surname and which was, with a slight alteration, the name of the region he originated from. Shortly after his marriage in 1711 to the daughter of one of the Duke of Gramont's Swiss mercenaries, he became a forester on the royal farms. His children married into good Parisian middle-class families; his son, Jean-Pierre-Henry, Parisian master merchant weaver, married the daughter of one of his colleagues, founding a dynasty of merchant weavers which stretched through the whole of the eighteenth century. Gustave Eiffel remained closely attached to his simultaneously bourgeois and artisan origins, emphasizing in his ancestors the love of a job well done and the tradition handed down from father to son: "Furthermore, the tapestry weaver's profession was an élite trade; it has left us, in that delicate branch of the art of furnishing, delightful patterns which we admire and still copy today as one of the most precious products of French taste. The weavers of that period, one of the most brilliant in the eighteenth century, were true artists."

"In our family," he again emphasized with pride, "there were in the eighteenth century ten master weavers."[2] Doubtless the source of the keen taste Eiffel had for eighteenth-century art, and for tapestries in particular, of which he made a collection in his mansion in the Rue Rabelais, must be seen in these distant origins, for the engineer's father broke with tradition and settled in the provinces.

This dynasty ended with Alexandre Eiffel, Gustave's father, born in 1795, who preferred the career of a soldier to the peaceful life of an artisan. In 1811, at the age of sixteen, he enlisted in the fifth regiment of lancers or hussars of Bercheny, serving with Eugène de Beauharnais in three Italian campaigns. When he was demobilized at the Restora-

tion, he held the position of adjutant. From 1820 to 1822, he was at the college at Saumur, which he remembered as the happiest time of his life. "He wrote in his own hand," noted his son, "a series of volumes reproducing some of the courses he took. These books, admirably written, are reverently preserved in my library."[3]

In 1823, Alexandre Eiffel was reinstated to the rank of adjutant; the following year, when garrisoned at Dijon, he left the service and married the daughter of a timber merchant, Catherine Mélanie Moneuse. It is tempting to say that Alexandre Eiffel remained a soldier in spirit. This is eloquently witnessed by his constant memory of the Napoleonic campaigns, his avowed Bonapartism, the military education he gave his son, and his distaste for business, which he left to his wife.

Madame Eiffel had a formative influence on her son. A masterful woman, she educated him, supervised him, set him up in business, and arranged his marriage; for any student of the great engineer's origins, the long and regular correspondence which she kept up with him until her death in 1878 is a source of primary importance.[4] In it she shows herself to be attentive, sometimes overly officious, always anxious, watching over his connections and pressing him to find a steady position. But this sometimes unflattering portrait of a committed mother, prone to nagging and making trouble, should not make us forget that Catherine Eiffel was the mainspring of her family's prosperity and that her incessant work made her son's education possible. The birth of Gustave in 1832 radically changed the life-style of the young couple. Hitherto they had been able to live modestly with the Moneuses, thanks to Alexandre Eiffel's salary as first secretary to the military *sous-intendant* at Dijon, a civil post which he had taken on leaving the army (in 1832 he was working in the Prefecture of the Côte d'Or). At that point Madame Eiffel looked for "some commercial employment, which would provide the opportunity to open up a wider and more lucrative field for her energy and her remarkable business sense."[5] She turned to the coal trade and secured the position of sole warehouseman of the Epinac mines for the city of Dijon

and the adjoining regions, such as the Haute-Marne, which, with its recently built blast furnaces, was then undergoing a considerable industrial expansion. Years later Gustave Eiffel paid tribute to his mother's business genius:

Right at the canal port she set up large coal depots, which were regularly restocked by a succession of overland deliveries. A great bustle pervaded these depots and my father soon had to give up his place in the Prefecture to join my mother, alongside whom his time was more usefully spent. My young imagination was deeply impressed by their strenuous labor to expedite the unloading of ships and the loading of carts, whatever the weather, which obliged them to leave the little house they lived in, on the very bank of the canal, at daybreak and which did not stop until after nightfall.

For their own use they had built a series of boats of which the first was called *Le beau Gustave* ("Gustave the Handsome") and the second *La petite Marie* ("Little Mary"), the name of my sister.

Thanks to hard work and the sense of order which animated them, their business prospered so much that at the end of eleven years, in 1843, they had by energy and thrift acquired a capital of about 300,000 francs, which at that time represented a comfortable private income of 15,000 francs a year; this allowed them to take their ease and quietly enjoy the fruits of their labors.

At that point my mother was so overcome with this very unexpected outcome that she allowed herself to be unsettled by a few small losses and bank failures; along with my father, she judged that they would be prudently advised to stop there, before their luck turned, and sell their commercial enterprise, for which they had received good offers.[6]

Giving up the coal trade, the Eiffels invested part of their new fortune in the business of a Dijon brewer, Edouard Régneau, whose tenants they became at Le Castel, a small eighteenth-century château where they lived until 1865.

It is hard to define the place which Alexandre and Catherine Eiffel occupied in the Dijon society of their day. In an ancien régime town like Dijon, where the nineteenth century had left only a late and peripheral impression (on Place Darcy and the area around the station), the Eiffels were simply *nouveaux riches* among the noble parliamentarian families which made up the core of society, despite the lengthy middle-class Parisian lineage which they could lay claim to.

At least this was evidently the information which reached Bordeaux when Gustave was trying to marry into good society there. Madame de Grangent's refusal to give him her daughter's hand and the reasons which she put forward concerning the social position of his family mortified the Eiffels, who felt they were being looked down on: "If she were Duchess of no matter where, an eighteen-year-old blonde with an income of 100,000 livres, she could not have made more of a fuss."[7] In vain the Dijon attorney disseminated flattering reports among Bordeaux families:

> M. and Mme. Eiffel made their fortune in business; in Dijon they were warehousemen for the Epinac mines and they retired fifteen to eighteen years ago with about 300,000 francs.
>
> Today they live in a handsome property called Le Castel, which belongs to the brewer M. Régneau, to whom M. Eiffel is accountant; by virtue of capital loans he is also a partner to an unknown extent.
>
> In business they have always had the highest and best-deserved reputation for probity and loyalty, and I know them to be people of the greatest possible refinement.... Their fortune is irreproachably established and there is no danger of losses; it consists of mortgage debentures. Every year they make savings, which they invest in my practice....[8]

Their Parisian middle-class roots were spelled out in vain; the Grangents obviously found the Eiffels too upstart. With one setback following another, Gustave Eiffel gave up all plans of marriage in Bordeaux, asserting that the inhabitants of Dijon were malicious and "readily join in repeating all sorts of nonsense."[9]

Having aspired to the upper middle class, the humiliated young engineer settled for the notch below, the provincial middle class to which he then belonged: "I shall be satisfied with a girl with a medium-sized dowry and passable looks, but on the other hand with a good disposition and simplicity of taste"[10]—shortcomings and virtues which

he was to find in Marie Gaudelet, the grand-daughter of the brewer Edouard Régneau, who became his wife.

Childhood

The first years of Gustave Eiffel's life, from his birth on December 15, 1832, until he reached Paris in October 1850, were spent in Dijon, at that time the somewhat sleepy capital of Burgundy and in no way the great industrial city in which one might have liked to see the "iron wizard" grow up. It was a tranquil childhood, provincial in the good sense of the word, and obviously happy, if his retrospective recollections are to be believed. In the genealogical section of his *Biographie*, Eiffel gave prominence to a long chapter entitled "Biographical Memories of My Early Years." He tells us that these were years of which he kept "much sharper memories than of other times in my life."[11] He examined the distant memories of his earliest youth for indications of his brilliant future career. He did not then live with his parents, but with his Moneuse grandmother in the Rue Turgot, near the rampart which has now been demolished. "The Rue Turgot ... was a blind alley with no through way for vehicles. A long tunnel through the rampart drained the rainwater from the street. It was closed by a large sheet-iron door which was the delight of all the children because if you threw a stone at the door the reverberation would make a fantastic din."[12] Abutting the rampart, which was no longer used for anything but a promenade, there was an astonishing microcosm of Eiffel's whole later life. For there one found the hovel of a scholar "with eccentric habits" of whom young Eiffel did not know "whether he was an alchemist or a student of sorcery"; there was a dressmaking workshop; the apartment of his uncle M. Mollerat, an able chemist; an infant school whose gymnastic equipment, swings, and pas de géant,* fascinated the young boy; a piece of waste ground called the yard which "was used as a supply depot for contractors' plant and materials"; a joiner's workshop; two handsome private houses inhabited by

---

* A piece of gymnastic apparatus: a mast with ropes attached, round which one can swing with long strides—Trans.

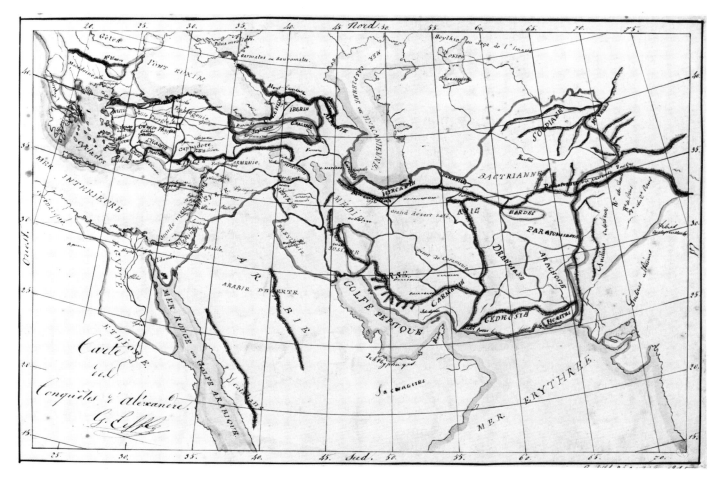

11   Gustave Eiffel, *Map of Alexander's Conquests*, 1845, pen and watercolor, Paris, Musée d'Orsay, Eiffel collection.

a class of people who were not on speaking terms with the Eiffels, the Mollerats, or the Moneuses; and, finally, a huge secularized convent.[13] In brief, it was a world which, writ large, would later be that of the entrepreneur: the world of the workshop, the builder's yard, and the luxurious, aristocratic home. As a small boy he lived with his blind grandmother, read her the Divine Office, slept by her in a little bed set up in her sleeping alcove, and went out every Sunday for a walk with his father. His first years of schooling—he attended junior classes in the neighborhood—left him nothing but "the most wretched memories," as did the following years spent in high school. "The student had to get quite far on (at least into the fourth grade and the classical form) to be able to find anything attractive in those dreary classes, in which you were unspeakably bored and felt you were completely wasting your time. All those years in school, with their

impositions,* detentions, their misuse of lessons learned by heart, the disgust at sessions in cold, dark, smelly rooms (like those of the Dijon high school) left the most dismal impression on my mind."[14] It was only during his last two years at school that Gustave Eiffel admitted to having learned anything, taking his two baccalauréats in humanities and in science.

After giving due emphasis to young Eiffel's prophetic interest in mechanical instruments and scenes of industrial life, a place must be made, right from his childhood in Dijon, for two scientific figures who played an important part in his development, Michel Perret and his "Uncle Mollerat."

Michel Perret was "a very distinguished chemist, who owned mines around Lyons that produced copper sulfide; this went under the generic name of pyrites and, when heated in controlled conditions,

---

* A task imposed as a result of poor work or bad behavior— Trans.

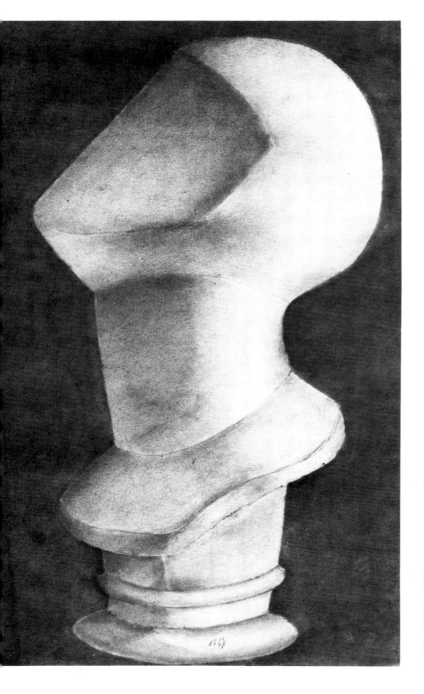 

produced sulfurous acid gas, which was converted into liquid sulfuric acid and air."[15] Eiffel often went with him into the various "lead chambers" around Dijon which belonged to him and where the acid was made by the slow and expensive process of burning the natural sulfur. Thanks to the expansion of this industry, of which he owned the virtual monopoly in France, Michel Perret achieved a position of the first rank in the business world and later became president of Saint-Gobain. But for the time being he took the young boy in hand, talking with him of "extraordinary things such as mesmerism, which he practiced on his servant, or philosophical themes such as theological arguments or the theories of Saint-Simon."[16]

Jean-Baptiste Mollerat, "Uncle Mollerat," brother of Eiffel's mother, was also an "eminent chemist" whom Eiffel, in his youth, held "in lively

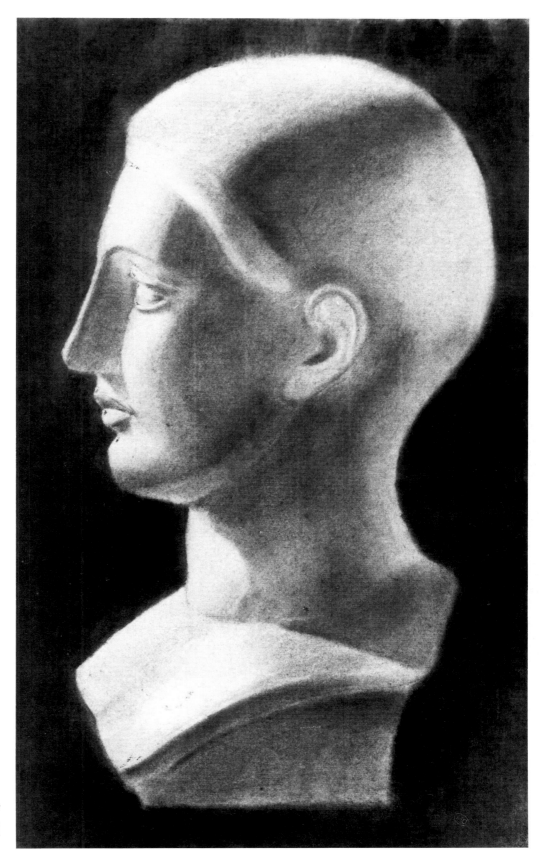

12–14 Gustave Eiffel, *Three studies of a bust*, charcoal, Paris, Musée d'Orsay, Eiffel collection.

15 Gustave Eiffel, *Bowl of fruit*, "M. Ernette's method, second lesson, December 6, 1847," pencil, Paris, Musée d'Orsay, Eiffel collection.

admiration". This man of eighteenth-century sympathies, a neighbor of Madame Moneuse, worthy according to his lights but authoritarian if not despotic, readily welcomed his enthusiastic nephew into the house near the rampart and into the great reception room in his factory at Pouilly-sur-Saône "where there was always a large number of people."[17] He was esteemed not only as a man of science but in addition as the friend of distinguished revolutionaries, a man "who had seen Robespierre guillotined." Of pronounced republican views, he emphatically repeated to his young nephew Gustave, "Make sure you remember, son,

that all kings are rogues." This scarcely pleased the Bonapartist Eiffel family and a few years later was at the root of a far-reaching quarrel.

At Pouilly, Mollerat had set up a factory for the distillation of wood in retorts for the production of "Mollerat vinegar" and "Mollerat green". The latter was "a highly resistant light green color which was used to paint shutters, plant containers, etc. ... This preparation was very successful and made the factory highly profitable, assuring him a very comfortable living. When he had achieved this he thought of retiring and handing his factory over to two of his nephews. But they were incapable of carrying on his work. Prosperity disappeared, and Uncle Mollerat was forced, at the age of seventy, to take up his business again and go back to work in order to avoid seeing it fail. Under his impetus it almost immediately began to prosper again, and he did not stop making large profits

28

until his death in 1855."[18] It was during the time when he was back in business that Eiffel knew him. The family ties as well as the close sympathy between uncle and nephew led Jean-Baptiste Mollerat at one point to name Gustave Eiffel as his successor to head the Pouilly-sur-Saône factory. With this in mind the young man specialized in chemistry at the Ecole Centrale (State School of Civil Engineering).

The influence of Perret and Mollerat was deep and enduring. To them the engineer owed his lack of religion (which did not stop him from attending church on special occasions, such as weddings or funerals), for in these two men who were his first teachers "there was not much room for divine law and revealed religion. However, under the influence of a liberal-minded priest named Father Louvot, I did show some fervor at the time of my first communion, but it was not to last; as Auguste Comte said and as one of my grandmother's boarders explained to me some years later, I had passed through the theological phase appropriate to the early development of the human spirit."[19] Some years later, when he was obstinately trying to get married in Bordeaux, Eiffel showed no sign of a better frame of mind. When a priest introduced him in proper form to the hostile family, he pretended to be deeply religious but could not help admitting to his mother that "the whole household thinks me a little saint and would be dumbfounded if they discovered the impropriety, religiously speaking, of my behavior."[20]

The Formative Years

At the beginning of October 1850, Gustave Eiffel left for Paris with his father. In order to study for the Polytechnic, the young man became a boarder at the Sainte Barbe Institute in the Latin Quarter. Paris was not unknown to him. He had already been there in 1844 and had been dazzled by "the brightness of the lights in the broadwalk of the Jardin des Plantes and in the Véro-Dodat arcade"; he had gotten to know the theaters and had looked around everywhere, under the spell of a "fairytale" city, which had an "indescribable" effect on him.[21] The idea of returning and eventually living there had rooted itself in his mind. A little later Madame Eiffel wrote, "Gustave dreams of nothing but Paris"; yet in spite of the family and the connections with Paris she was always suspicious of the capital.[22] In 1848, finding himself in the stolid middle-class calm of Dijon, Eiffel had regretted not being able to take part in the revolutionary events, other than by reading of them in the papers, which allowed him to relive in detail the vicissitudes of that troubled spring: "I was there, I sat in at the session; there in front of me Barbès gesticulated on the rostrum, there Cabet and Blanqui mounted it in their turn and others followed them. I saw it all, I heard it all."[23] But after he went to college his tone was less enthusiastic: "This is the first letter I am sending you from Sainte Barbe," he wrote to his mother on October 12, 1850, "which makes quite an impression on me. I have been settled in since yesterday and, after some annoyances and some removal problems, here I am sitting at an oak table blackened by the rubbing of many elbows; I am in a classroom which is cold and quiet and almost empty; I can see nothing except the many windows of the building and the black walls of the Collège Louis-le-Grand, instead of the lovely view I used to have from my window and so I am sad in spite of myself. Nothing is arranged yet; we have nothing to do; I am bored. In the midst of all these strangers, whom I have not had time to get to know, I think about Dijon and all the folks I have left there."[24]

This captivity lasted for only two years and was broken by frequent outings and regular journeys to Dijon. The free days "are almost all spent in going to the Louvre or to the Conservatoire des Arts et Métiers,"[25] or else strolling along the boulevards, going to mesmerism séances, to see a play, or to visit his Parisian correspondents, the Denis family.

The first year, Gustave Eiffel failed his examinations; in the second, he was only allowed to sit for the written examination for the Polytechnic, but this gave him the right to a place in the Ecole Centrale des Arts et Manufactures, which was less prestigious but offered a more industrial vocation than the Ecole Polytechnique. The grades he earned during those three years were varied, but always poor in drawing, which was a real obstacle to him: "My only nightmare is drawing, I think the teacher gives me bad marks out of habit."[26] In the second year, when he had to specialize and choose between metallurgy, mechanics, civil engineering, or chemistry, he opted for the last with the idea of succeeding his uncle Mollerat in the factory at

Pouilly-sur-Saône. But soon afterwards a family quarrel arose which Eiffel described in detail in his *Biographie*, for it was for him "the cause of a complete change of career" and for his family "the failure to share in a large inheritance."[27] The somewhat slender occasion of it was the liberty which a young chemist called Boutin, a graduate of the Ecole Centrale, had taken with Gustave's sister Marie, to whom he had just become engaged. "M. Boutin," explained Eiffel, "got on well with everybody except my father, who had Bonapartist sympathies whereas those of M. Boutin were openly republican." Alexandre Eiffel, who did not look favorably on this marriage, used the pretext of a stolen kiss to make a fuss and turn the suitor out. His brother-in-law Mollerat took the affair very badly and demanded apologies which were not forthcoming. The two families quarreled and never saw one another again. Boutin disappeared. Uncle Mollerat died the following year without leaving any trace, while the factory, taken over by one of his nieces, went progressively downhill. "The plant from the Pouilly factory was scattered and sold like old scrap. All the buildings were demolished and the site given over to cultivation. So the plough was driven over this factory where the industrial genius of one man had created a source of wealth for the surrounding area as well as for himself."[28]

In this way the dream of a peaceful career as a chemist was brutally brought to an end. When he left the Ecole Centrale with his chemical engineering diploma in his pocket, Eiffel had to busy himself finding a job. Thinking of turning to metallurgy, he asked advice from his brother-in-law Joseph Collin, his sister Laure's husband, who was manager of the blast furnaces in the foundry at Châtillon-sur-Seine. On September 7, 1855, he explained the situation to his mother at great length and in terms which, in retrospect, make us smile: "It is clear that I do not understand a great deal about metallurgy, so I must of necessity spend some time at an apprenticeship, by the end of which I should certainly be in a much more favorable position to find a place somewhere, keeping in mind that more is demanded in a private enterprise than in some public service or other; so, if this apprenticeship is indispensable, I would be better placed at Châtillon than anywhere else." There remained the question of his position in relation to his brother-in-law: "On the other hand, Joseph

would like me to start here without terms, except for payment on completion of the work for any services I may render. The reason for this is as follows: a salary would perforce tie me to one special area of mechanics, which would not allow me to follow the business as a whole."[29]

So Gustave Eiffel made his start in metallurgy as a voluntary collaborator with his brother-in-law, apprehensive like all beginners, anxious to see everything, the technical as well as the financial aspects, himself setting a limit to this probationary period: "It is by no means certain what use I shall be," he commented to his mother, "but at least I am playing my small part without being pulled up too often. Nevertheless, I have always thought, like you, that this position should have a date put on it and I had settled on January 1. Also I have several projects in hand which I am going to push ahead and which I shall certainly have worked out by that time."[30]

At the beginning of 1856, he accordingly left Châtillon for Paris and introduced himself to Charles Nepveu, a railway construction engineer who had a business at 36 Rue de la Bienfaisance: "Steam engine building, tools, forge, boilerworks, boiler-plate works, railroad rolling stock, and permanent way: Nepveu and Co." Nepveu had his workshops in the Quartier Saint-Augustin, which today is inhabited predominantly by the middle class but which at that time, known by the name of Little Poland, was almost deserted, being visited only by a few ragpickers. There was also an annex at Clichy which was concerned in a more specialized way with the production of railroad cars. The meeting between Nepveu and Eiffel was a determining factor in the young engineer's career, "which," he was to note later, "he followed without turning aside, that professional continuity becoming his principal rule of behavior."[31]

At a salary of 150 francs a month, Eiffel became Charles Nepveu's private secretary "to study the questions which M. Nepveu was preoccupied with, notably that of foundations in rivers, concerning which he had already assembled many documents which were to be presented at a convocation of civil engineers."[32] He worked extremely hard, learning

16 Chanmoit?, *"Eiffel the engineer testing his invention for an inexplosive engine, February 3, 1856,"* pencil and pastel, Paris, Musée d'Orsay, Eiffel collection.

L'ingénieur L... faisant l'essai d'une locomotive inexplosible
de son invention. —

techniques which he would have occasion to use a little later in the Bordeaux bridge, and those over the Nive, the Garonne, and finally over the Dordogne at Floirac. This process, later replaced by using the "weight of the beton infill in the external metal shell," involved "transferring, by means of hydraulic presses, the action of the counterweight back to the heads of the tubes which made up the piles. The action of this counterweight served either to resist the internal pressure due to compressed air or to overcome the friction of the earth against the piles as they were driven in."[33]

Nepveu treated Eiffel as a friend, left him free to make himself familiar with all the files, and introduced him to important scientific figures, such as Léon Molinos, the future president of the Société des Ingénieurs Civils, Emile Trélat, professor at the Conservatoire des Arts et Métiers and founder of the Ecole Spéciale d'Architecture, and de Dion, who directed the difficult restoration work on the main tower of Bayeux Cathedral. Eiffel was fired with enthusiasm and devoted all his time to his new employer: "Every morning I am there by 8:15 at the latest; at 10:45 I go out for lunch and I have to be back by noon to talk to M. Nepveu, who finishes lunch then. I go out for dinner at 5:45. Perhaps you think I have finished then, but no! Except on Mondays, when M. Nepveu has his friends in, he makes me come almost every evening to work with him until 11 o'clock or midnight. He is, moreover, a tireless worker himself. As for Sundays, I shall take a special course with M. Le Play, a teacher at the Ecole des Mines.... In spite of this, I am highly satisfied at getting a job with him. If I stay here I am sure of my future; whatever happens he is going to take me through so many things that I am bound to gain enormously."[34]

Contrary to Eiffel's expectations, Charles Nepveu's affairs suddenly took a downward turn. In May 1856, he suspended payments and disappeared. Bad deals, insufficient capital for unduly heavy undertakings, and sluggish returns were the cause of the collapse. But on May 30, Nepveu, whose conduct was nothing if not strange, reappeared, brought back from Geneva by Trélat. There was none of the explanations to which Eiffel was entitled, but a joyful reunion: "We hugged one another with the feelings of friends of twenty years' standing."[35] The business went into liquidation and Nepveu was appointed administrator for the liquidation, while Eiffel agreed to stay with him

voluntarily for a while. "Thanks to that," he immediately wrote to his mother, trying vainly both to reassure her and to soften her heart, "we are bound to each other and I assure you that he is a man of means.... Besides, I feel that my fate is bound up with M. Nepveu's and he sees it the same way."[36] Nepveu took pains to find a place for his protégé and on August 1 Eiffel joined the Compagnie des chemins de fer de l'Ouest, an important concern which owned the Gare St. Lazare and combined the companies of Le Havre, Rouen, Dieppe, Caen, Saint-Germain, and the two Versailles railroads. Eiffel met again a departmental head whom he had known at the Ecole Centrale and continued to work at full stretch. "I am engaged at the railroad office from 9:00 A.M. to 5:30 P.M., and I have a great deal of work there. Thanks to M. Nepveu, who comes to speak for me and find out what they are giving me to do, I am very well regarded and I am only set interesting tasks. I am now planning a sheet-metal bridge and I study almost every evening with my boss. We work together until midnight or 1 A.M. I continue to visit M. Nepveu no less assiduously, which takes up every moment I have left. Several times already I have left his house at 10 P.M. and gone to work with my departmental head, with whom I am going to have even more important things to study."[37] Gustave Eiffel's first design, a 22-meter cast- and sheet-iron bridge for the Saint-Germain railroad, was accepted in September.

At the end of October, he announced to his mother that, with a former boss, he was studying "the design of a very big bridge." This was the beginning of his work on what was to be the Bordeaux bridge."[38] At the same time Nepveu was negotiating the transfer of his factory to a Belgian group. The negotiations were concluded in December. The limited company directed by the Belgian industrialists Pauwels, who were railroad car and general railroad constructors, bought the Paris and Clichy factories for a very high price in order to expand their own facilities. Nepveu became the managing director, at a substantial salary, and kept control of the Paris factories. "In other words," Eiffel summed up, "the limited partnership of which he was the head has grown bigger, acquired fresh capital, and changed into a limited company."[39] Rather than linking Eiffel with himself again as private secretary, which would have put him in a precarious position, since he would have been entirely dependent on the fate of his employer, Nepveu put him into the business directed by François Pauwels, as head of the research department at the Paris factories. This was a position which delighted Eiffel; he had regarded his previous job in the Compagnie des chemins de fer de l'Ouest only as "a temporary place, a sort of inn where you put up while you are waiting for something better."[40] The something better had arrived. It allowed him to settle in Paris and look forward to the future in an easier frame of mind. He was no longer dependent on a boss–an enterprising one, full of ideas, it was true, but unrealistic; instead he had a steady job in a prosperous business.

Eiffel was to regret leaving the Compagnie des chemins de fer de l'Ouest still less when, in July 1857, following a series of intrigues, Flachat, the chief engineer, whom he knew well and thought highly of, was dismissed and replaced by a bridge builder. In the process all the staff were discharged. A little later Nepveu, in negotiations with the Compagnie du Midi, obtained for Pauwels the commission to build the Bordeaux bridge, which was to link up the rail network of the Compagnie d'Orléans with that of the Compagnie du Midi. He immediately entrusted the execution of the work to his protégé.

17 *Gustave Eiffel c. 1860*, watercolor, Paris, Musée d'Orsay, Eiffel collection.

The Early Works

The work on the Bordeaux bridge (1858–60) was a determining stage in Eiffel's career. The project stood out by virtue of its strategic importance: it would connect two hitherto separate rail networks. (The Paris–Bordeaux railroad ended at the Gare de La Bastide, on the right bank of the Garonne; the lines from Sète to Bordeaux and Bayonne to Bordeaux were operated by the Pereire brothers of the Compagnie des chemins de fer du Midi, whose terminus was on the left bank, at the Gare du Midi.) Equally, it would save time and money by avoiding the expensive unloading and reloading of goods and by saving travelers the need to cross the old stone bridge, on foot or by carriage, to reach the other bank. On the other hand it presented a real structural challenge: establishing six 25-meter piers in the turbulent waters by means of compressed air ("one of the first major applications of this method of laying foundations") and setting up a metal superstructure 500 meters long. For his "business début," Eiffel was given important assignments, including "the whole assemblage of the metal section, which was carried out on site in workshops specially built for the purpose."[41] In fact, the young engineer took over progressively from Nepveu (whose behavior was becoming stranger and stranger; he finally resigned on March 31, 1860), and at the age of twenty-six was responsible for overseeing the whole site, including "construction work in the river, service bridges, compressed air foundations, and the manufacture and assembly of the metal superstructure."[42]

To the Pauwelses' great satisfaction, Eiffel "came through the job which had devolved upon him with flying colors and completed the work within the agreed two-year time span."[43] In spite of the solicitous presence of his sister Marie and the efficient help of his brother-in-law Armand Hussonmorel, the supervision of the work often put the young engineer to the test. He had to solve most of the problems on his own (the gradual sinking of the service bridge, difficulties in providing the building materials). But in the letters written to his parents (the lonelier he felt, the more frequent they were), he often wrote of successes. In December 1858, he sent his father a photograph of the wooden service bridge, taken from 300 meters upstream "to show you that your son, bad engineer though you may think him, still knows how to stack a fair number of cubic meters of wood, about 1,800 of them, in quite a short time."[44] A year later he went to Strasbourg to see the important work on the Kehl bridge, which was talked of much more than that of the Bordeaux bridge. "We make less of a show than they do," he commented, "but in spite of their success I also believe that our system is better: only they are throwing a bit of money out of the window and dazzling everybody."[45]

One of Eiffel's main preoccupations was to assure his future after Bordeaux. In 1859, he talked to his mother about distant plans for a bridge over the Vistula and a railroad in the Caucasus, but he hesitated: "Afterwards I shouldn't know where to go; I should much prefer to go and direct another big scheme than return to Paris where I don't see any suitable openings at the moment."[46] He was the more worried for seeing a difficult future for metallurgy, finding that "the trade was being spoiled" (this he repeated, at intervals, throughout his life), and thinking that if he "had any capital" he would not venture it in "metal bridges or in embankments."[47] On the Bordeaux site it was once again Eiffel's luck to meet men who appreciated his skill and would entrust other business to him. In this way Stanislas de La Roche-Tolay, the engineer who had worked with him on the plans for the bridge and who would continue "to take the most friendly interest in him for many more years,"[48] gave him other jobs for the Compagnie des chemins de fer du Midi, notably the bridge over the Nive at Bayonne, which also had

18 *The Bordeaux Bridge* (1858–60), photograph published by Eiffel in his *Biographie industrielle et scientifique*, vol. 1, Paris, Musée d'Orsay, Eiffel collection.

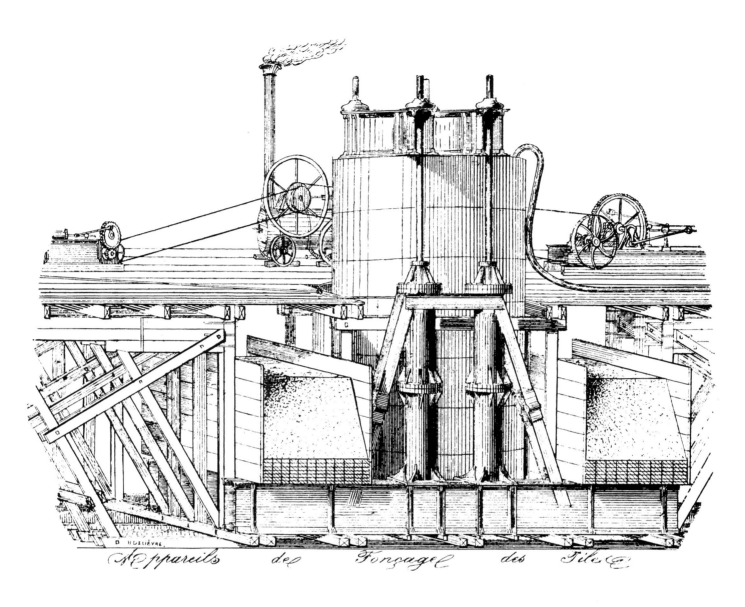

Appareils de Fonçage des Piles

compressed air foundations. Eiffel undertook them in the workshops set up at La Bastide for the construction of the Bordeaux bridge.

It was through La Roche-Tolay that Eiffel met Jean-Baptiste Krantz (then working for the Compagnie d'Orléans at Périgueux on the opening up of the central network) and his subordinate, his brother-in-law Duval. "They placed complete trust in M. Eiffel and negotiated with him the execution of several contracts, among others the bridges of Capdenac on the Lot, and Floirac on the Dordogne."[49] Another engineer, Léon Courras, general secretary of the central network of the Compagnie d'Orléans, introduced Eiffel to Wilhelm Nordling, who was then designing the metal viaducts on the line between Commentry and

19 Pile-driving equipment used by Eiffel at the time of the building of the Bordeaux bridge, engraving published in the *Biographie industrielle et scientifique*, vol. 1, p. 3 bis, Paris, Musée d'Orsay, Eiffel collection.

Gannat, and who remembered the young engineer a few years later at the time when they were built.

The period stretching from the completion of the site work in July 1860 (on that occasion Eiffel was presented with a medal by his workforce), to the setting up of the engineering workshops in Levallois-Perret in 1866 was an unsettled one (one might readily call it a "period of transition" if that expression had not been overused). It saw Gustave Eiffel steadily gain a high reputation in the industrial world, successfully carry out several important undertakings—and a certain number of minor ones—and multiply his projects right up to the start of the Eiffel Company at the end of 1866. On the site at Bordeaux, which, despite his lack of experience, he had managed admirably, he had shown qualities as an organizer and leader of men which were subsequently acknowledged everywhere. The Pauwelses could only be grateful to him and, in September 1860, appointed him engineer general to the railroad construction company, subordinate only to the administrative board and the management in Brussels, with an annual salary of 9,000 francs and a 5 percent share in the projects he directed; if the company wanted to terminate his contract he was to be given a year's notice. In 1862, the net profit on the business he had conducted was 58,650 francs, "an even more creditable performance since the Brussels factory has made little profit this year and the one at Paris none at all."[50] The consolidation of his place at the heart of the Belgian firm was the more opportune because his connections with Nepveu were weakening, until they finally came to an end in 1861. He then learned from the Pauwelses of "several rather disagreeable characteristics of M. Nepveu's"[51] and declared that he was pleased to have broken off from him. Nevertheless, at the end of his life, when he was paying tribute to the people who had helped him most at the start, he named Nepveu first and foremost: "So it is in large part to M. Nepveu and to the three engineers M. de La Roche-Tolay, M. Krantz, and M. Duval that M. Eiffel owed the success of his first undertakings, for which he has always remained very grateful."[52]

Eiffel continued his progress with the Pauwelses and became "more and more the man the company relied on."[53] The directors would have liked to see him installed with them in Brussels, but that scarcely tempted him—still less so when, in July 1862, having unsuccessfully proposed to four well-dowried girls within one year, he finally married. His bride, settled for in due form by his mother, Madame Eiffel, was the granddaughter of the good M. Régneau, Marie Gaudelet; she had acceptable looks and only a modest fortune, but was clearly gifted with an excellent disposition. It was to be one of the happiest marriages, which led to the birth of several children, until its sad end, with the death of Marie Eiffel, in 1877. The loving and self-effacing young wife, whom we glimpse

through her letters to her in-laws, did not complain too much about her husband's continual absence. Eiffel, exhausted, unburdened himself to his mother about it: "Although I am not a knight, I am no less errant, and the firm makes me earn my salary by the number of miles it forces me to cover. Since my wedding I have not managed to have a few days' peace.... During the last week I have been to Toulouse, Paris, and Bayonne and, what is worse, I am leaving again on Sunday for Spain, where they are expecting me at Santander."[54] It was a journey which then took fifty or sixty hours by train.

The reward for so many trials was not long in coming. In the fall of 1862, Eiffel was appointed, at a salary of 12,000 francs per annum, director of the company's workshops at Clichy. In December, he settled down there in a large house, 3 Rue du Port. But in 1863, the company's affairs began to go progressively downhill with the workshops turning out only a few orders for metal bridges. At first Eiffel was little worried; the industrial crisis seemed to him to be a general phenomenon, in short, a bad time to get through. In spite of hopes for deals in Italy and Turkey (which came to nothing), by May the situation had become alarming. There was a 300,000 franc loss at Clichy, where the monthly overhead of 45,000 francs demanded a turnover of four to five million francs a year.[55] Beginning in November, Eiffel was obliged to lay off employees although it cost him dearly. He tried to pull through in another way, by distancing himself from the Pauwelses, and in this way, in February 1864, he managed to take over from the railroad construction company the building of the station concourse at Toulouse and at Agen, two deals which he completed during 1865. In September, Eiffel had a final meeting with his boss: "No good came out of my discussions with M. Pauwels. The company is at the end of its resources; 500-franc shares stand at 175 francs, and they are trying to accomplish the difficult task of meeting obligations with an exhausted credit. In short, it is for the moment a more or less dead enterprise, and the best thing would be to get out of it as soon as possible to avoid being entangled in all the delights of a liquidation. So I did not agree to accept a post as consultant engineer at a reduced salary, which would have been a short-lived sinecure, and I prefer to make my own arrangements for the settlement of the compensation due to me."[56] Nevertheless, they parted on the best of terms. Pauwels promised to take Eiffel on again if he established a new business. Eiffel set up on his own as a consulting engineer, not too worried about the immediate future, thanks to the orders from Toulouse and Agen and the prospect of a flourishing business with Egypt. In fact, the Egyptian government wanted thirty-three 8-horsepower locomotives, to be built completely in France. Eiffel explained: "I shall have only to supervise their manufacture in Paris, which will not take me much time; all my expenses will be paid and, over and above that, I shall have a 25 percent share in the profits. The profits will very probably reach about 40,000 francs, which will give me at least 10,000 francs as my share, without great labor and quite without risk."[57] This contract, which continued through 1865, obliged him to go to Egypt, where he visited Cairo, Alexandria, the isthmus, and Memphis. Above all he collected some notes on the Suez Canal, which he promised himself he would publish on his return and which he recalled twenty years later when he began thinking about the Panama Canal.

The other important business which was begun before Eiffel set up at Levallois-Perret was the building of the exhibition hall for the 1867 Universal Exhibition. He announced that he would take part in this large state commission immediately after the appointment of Krantz, with whom he had collaborated as works manager on the bridges of the central rail network. Since Eiffel still had no workshops in action, Krantz could only entrust him with technical assistance. His job was to "draw up designs for the arch-girders of the Galerie des Machines—let us only remember that the gigantic hall, built in 1867 on the Champ de Mars by Le Play and Krantz, was made up of concentric galleries, enclosing a central garden, in which products were conscientiously, though not effectively, distributed by category and by country of origin—as well as the theoretical research for these arches and the experimental verification of his calculations."[58] In a memoir, Eiffel drew the lessons from the experiments on spanning arches which he had made in the Gouin workshops. He established for the first time the value (subsequently agreed everywhere) of the "modulus of elasticity applicable to the compound castings which go to make up metal structures."[59] Beyond the technical cooperation "which he gave unstintingly to M. J. B. Krantz," Eiffel's involvement in this second Universal Exhibition in Paris was restricted to "a few unimportant pieces of work like the Galerie des Beaux-Arts et d'Archéologie which made up the central part of the exhibition."[60]

Unable to conclude a good bargain with Krantz because he had no workshop, Eiffel had to hurry things along. At the end of 1866, thanks to a twelve-year loan from Edouard Régneau, he moved into a block of workshops at 48 Rue Fouquet in Levallois-Perret. From December 4, in a handbill under the name of "Gustave Eiffel, builder," enumerating his various "specialisms … iron constructions, market halls and builders' hardware, reservoirs, gasholders, boilers, and in general all metal constructions," he appealed to his future clients as follows:

I have the honor to inform you that my workshops have been newly fitted up at Levallois near the Porte de Courcelles (Paris) and I beg you to have the goodness to include me among the contractors you usually ask to tender for work in boiler-making and any metal construction you may need.

The important projects of all kinds which I have directed, as engineer to the General Railroad Construction Company, or which I have carried out myself as contractor (the metal bridge at Bordeaux for the Compagnie du Midi, the bridges at Capdenac and Floirac for the Compagnie d'Orléans, the station concourses at Toulouse and Agen, and now the central galleries and internal canopies of the 1867 Universal Exhibition, etc.) allow me to hope that you will be good enough to take my request into consideration.[61]

Perhaps it was bold of him to claim that he was the contractor for the Bordeaux bridge, but what did that matter? The Eiffel business was born.

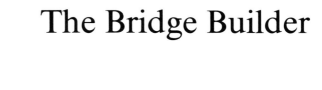

The Bridge Builder

The Eiffel Company

Levallois-Perret,[1] at first a village and then a town, had sprung from a scheme drawn up by Jean-Jacques Perret in 1822, and had been developed by Nicolas Levallois, who in 1846 sold 250 hectares as lots. By the 1860s, it was already a sizable place, where "warehouses for yeast, metal mirrors, paints, horseshoe nails, starch, ink, waterproof varnished paper, and railroad carriages, wagons, and equipment"[2] were to be found. The creation of the twenty arrondissements of Paris by Napoleon III and Haussmann in 1860, and the consequent removal of industry to the edge of the city, were unquestionably to the advantage of this nearby suburb; gradually the village would disappear, becoming an industrial zone built on a strict plan, though the scattered, ill-assorted buildings remained interspersed with little gardens, waste ground, and barely discernible paths. By 1880, Levallois-Perret had 30,000 inhabitants; it had 20,000 more in 1898, thus making it the most densely populated town in the department.

On October 6, 1868, two years after he had settled there, Gustave Eiffel formed a limited partnership which was to allow him to take on large-scale projects. His partner was Théophile Seyrig, a wealthy young civil engineer, who had left the Ecole Centrale in 1865. The company was established for a period of five years and the address of its registered office was that of the workshops: 48 rue Fouquet, Levallois-Perret. Gustave Eiffel was the sole signatory, and he alone had "the powers associated with the office of managing partner"; nevertheless, he might "delegate all or part of his powers to a representative of his choice who would act under his authority."[3] Seyrig might only ask him for employment in his establishment and could not lay claim to "any part in managing or directing the company". Eiffel was to receive 12,000 francs per year as manager's salary; he contributed the sum of 84,000 francs, consisting of "1) his customers and his trading contacts, estimated at 25,000 francs; 2) the whole of his trading assets, with all the debts and charges dependent thereon, the said assets comprising the whole of the moneys owing to him and his industrial equipment, such as steam-driven machines, machines for stamping large and small work, raw materials, goods already manufactured or in the process of manufacture, amounting to the total sum of 59,000 francs, as calculated from the inventory drawn up jointly by the two partners on 1 July last."

Seyrig, for his part, contributed the considerably larger sum of 126,000 francs in cash, which the manager was only to use when he needed it. Thus the total of the company's registered capital was 210,000 francs. Forty percent of the profits were to go to the management, represented by Eiffel, and sixty percent to the registered capital formed by the two partners' contributions; "this latter part shall itself be shared between the two partners according to the amount of their respective contributions."

The contract was extended for a further fifteen years on October 11, 1873, but on June 30, 1879, Eiffel, who had just been allocated the contract for the Garabit viaduct, parted company with Seyrig, who had become too greedy. In 1881–84, Seyrig entered into a protracted dispute over the splitting of the profits, gaining almost 800,000 francs from his eleven years of partnership with Gustave Eiffel.

From its establishment at Levallois-Perret in 1866 until it was put into liquidation in 1975, the company formed by Gustave Eiffel played a leading role in metal construction both in France and in the French colonies. We shall only deal with the works carried out before 1893, the date when Eiffel resigned from the board of directors (of which he had been chairman until then) after an extraordinary general meeting had decided to reduce the company's capital. Four years earlier the limited partnership G. Eiffel et Compagnie, formed with Théophile Seyrig in 1868, had become the Compagnie des Etablissements Eiffel, a new company to which Eiffel had contributed his Levallois-Perret workshops, his offices and agencies in the colonies and abroad, the patents he had obtained, and all the orders in production at the time. From 1895, the company was directed by Maurice Koechlin, one of Eiffel's main collaborators; it then dropped the name of its founder to become the Société de Construction de Levallois-Perret, a name which it retained until 1937, when it took up Eiffel's name again, becoming Anciens Etablissements Eiffel. In 1960, the name was changed to Etablissements Eiffel, and five years later to Société Eiffel.

Thanks to the documents preserved in the French National Archives in Paris,[4] we can gain a fairly good idea of the large quantity and the diversity of the work carried out by this company over more than 100 years. It should be noted, however, that these files are far from complete (the plans relating to the 300-meter tower, for example, belong to the Société Nouvelle d'Exploitation de la Tour Eiffel, the S.N.T.E.), since the National Archives had to make only a representative selection from the great mass of papers offered them when the liquidator handed over the files; thus they cannot provide a basis for an exhaustive list of the work carried out by Eiffel. Nevertheless, the size of orders, the general course of business, and the introduction of silent partners can be assessed. Although, with Eiffel as chairman of the board, large-scale constructions in big cities formed the majority of the company's activity until the beginning of the 1890s, this activity would subsequently become more diverse. In France large-scale work became rarer; on the other hand, the colonies called on French manufacturers for all their extensive infrastructural work: a branch in Madagascar and then one in Dakar were added to the one in Saigon. The real decline began after the First World War, when concrete rather than metal became the material of choice for infrastructural work, and the company formerly directed by Gustave Eiffel became primarily involved with the construction of industrial plant.

Eiffel may not have played a pioneering role in the use of metal, but he was a master of it, developing its applications and producing some structures which, by virtue of their size, their novelty, and their beauty, fully earned him the appellation "iron wizard," bestowed upon him by one of his first biographers.[5] In 1888, when he expounded the advantages of this material to the French Association for the Advancement of Science, and speaking principally of wrought iron (cast iron, being too brittle, was hardly used any longer, while steel, which he termed "the metal of the future," had yet to come into its own), Eiffel emphasized its strength—ten times the strength of wood, twenty times that of stone; its lightness, which, for example, made it possible for the load on the ground of the 300-meter tower which he was constructing to be roughly equal to that of a single Paris apartment block; and, finally, its elasticity, which enabled it to resist both tensile stresses and compression. He went on to enumerate all the great constructions erected during the nineteenth century, modestly giving his own works only a small place in this list.[6]

When talking of Eiffel, it is generally only a few of his major constructions which are mentioned (the tower, of course, the bridges in Portugal, the Garabit viaduct, the Statue of Liberty); the everyday work of the company he had formed is overlooked, though it was this work which made it possible for him to operate. Thus the demountable bridges which were always in stock at Levallois-Perret ensured continuous employment for the workshops and were to provide a fairly constant trade, at least until the First World War. Beginning in 1884, the company printed a catalogue of the "new, economic, Eiffel-system portable bridges, patented without government guarantee of quality, for use on country roads, in army campaigns, on narrow-gauge railroads, and roads in the colonies." In fact, these were designed to facilitate rapid establishment of communications—mainly in distant countries—for army campaigns or the needs of trade. As early as 1873, Eiffel had been concerned with this problem in relation to the bridges he had built in Bolivia, but it was only in 1879 that he began to study a particular type of metal bridge for army use. His starting point was a conversation with the governor of Cochin-China, Le Myre de Villers. The colony was crisscrossed with waterways, and Le Myre de Villers thought that there would be great advantages to be gained from making a very simple portable type of bridge, "which could be used with the same components for different spans, and which could easily be set up over the little arroyos which are found everywhere in this country."[7]

The task, although apparently simple, presented numerous difficulties. In effect, Eiffel had to devise a bridge that was easy to construct; it therefore had to comprise only a limited number of parts, each of which had to be easy to transport in countries with very few communication routes; which had to be light, so that it did not need major supports, but was also rigid; and which could be assembled with bolts rather than rivets, so that skilled workers would not be required. He therefore designed a steel bridge consisting of "two girders making up the parapets, with their lower chords joined by bridge members or supporting struts. These bridge members are joined together in turn by wire stringers which support the roadway. A windbrace completes the structure of the bridge. The basic idea of our system is that the girders are made up of a number of identical coplanar triangular components, placed back to back and joined together." The girders consisted of only three types of components: the longitudinal elements (absolutely indeformable isosceles triangles riveted in the workshop), the end posts (half a longitudinal element with a reinforced vertical), and the tie bars (a simple angle section which served as the lower chord of the girder). "To imagine a girder formed from these components, simply picture a certain number of them placed end to end, 1 B_2 4, 5 B_4 8, etc. (fig. 3, plate 1), and arranged so that all their angle sections are turned to the same side."[8]

This system clearly had many advantages: no more preliminary studies and plans designed specially for each commission; assembly that did not require skilled workers; easy positioning, by rolling out, and disassembly which was just as easy. Once established and patented, this system also did away with the delays usually encountered in obtaining approval of the project and putting it up for tender; and as they were always available at the workshop, individual parts were sent immediately upon request.

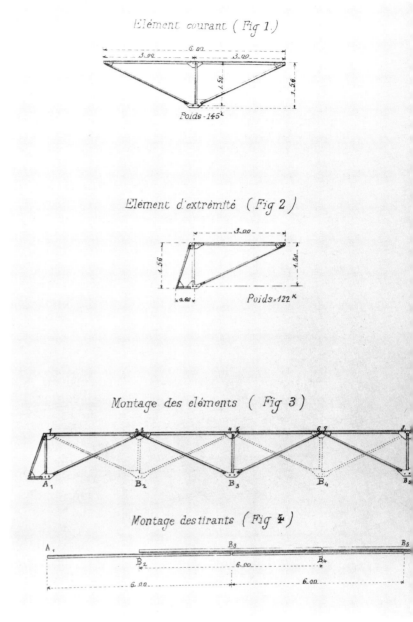

20 "New, Eiffel method, cheap portable bridges," plate 1, catalogue for 1885.

The different types of "economical portable bridges"—road bridges with wooden roadways; road bridges with metal roadways for metalled roads; military bridges for troops and artillery; bridges for movable railroads; bridges for one-meter-gauge railroads; bridges for the restoration of standard-gauge railroads; footbridges for pedestrians and pack animals—all these enjoyed

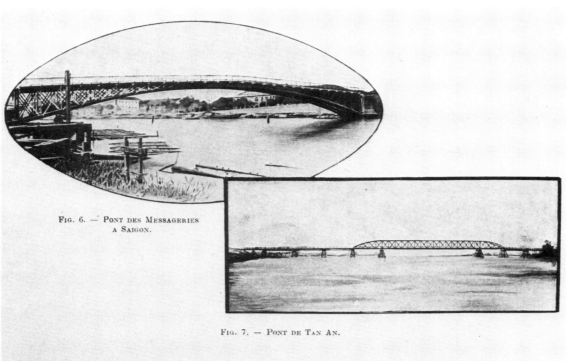

FIG. 6. — PONT DES MESSAGERIES
A SAIGON.

FIG. 7. — PONT DE TAN AN.

FIG. 8. — PONT DU TAGE.

FIG. 9. — PONT DE COBAS.

FIG. 10. — PONT DE VIANNA.

21 *Messageries Bridge at Saigon; bridge at Tan An; bridge over the Tagus; bridge at Cobas; bridge at Vianna,* plate from the *Biographie industrielle et scientifique,* vol. 1, Paris, Musée d'Orsay, Eiffel collection.

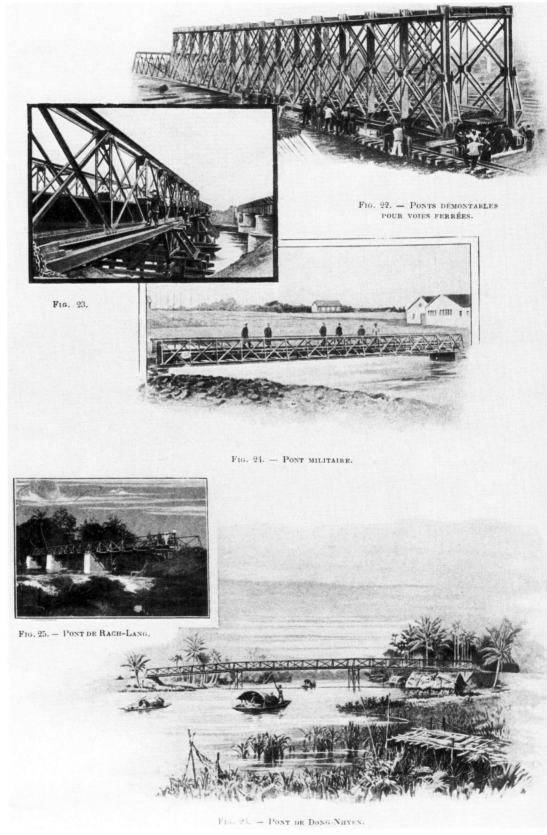

FIG. 22. — PONTS DÉMONTABLES POUR VOIES FERRÉES.

FIG. 23.

FIG. 24. — PONT MILITAIRE.

FIG. 25. — PONT DE RACH-LANG.

FIG. 25. — PONT DE DONG-NHYEN.

22 *Demountable railroad bridges; military bridge; bridge at Rach-Lang; bridge at Dong-Nhyen,* plate from the *Biographie industrielle et scientifique,* vol. 1, Paris, Musée d'Orsay, Eiffel collection.

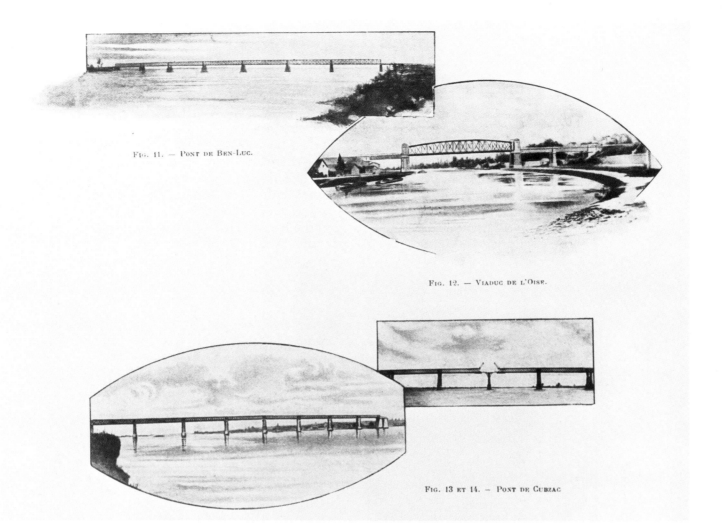

FIG. 11. — PONT DE BEN-LUC.

FIG. 12. — VIADUC DE L'OISE.

FIG. 13 ET 14. — PONT DE CUBZAC

A. CHARVET
TORINO
24 Aprile 1884

immediate success: the total length of those constructed was more than 10,000 meters. Both in France and abroad, many experiments were carried out on them: on February 1, 1882, at Levallois-Perret, a 4-tonne, single-axled carriage drawn by two horses crossed a 21-meter bridge several times without producing the slightest deformation in the deck; the same type of experiment was carried out on the Michelotti Canal bridge in Turin on April 22 and 24, 1884, and a series of photographs was taken which were widely reproduced. There are many letters testifying to the merits of the bridges, and the services they rendered. Edouard Clayeux, a farmer on the Gouttes estate in the Allier department, praised the 21-meter bridge he had had built on his land in 1883: "I finished cutting my hay, and I had more than eighty carts cross

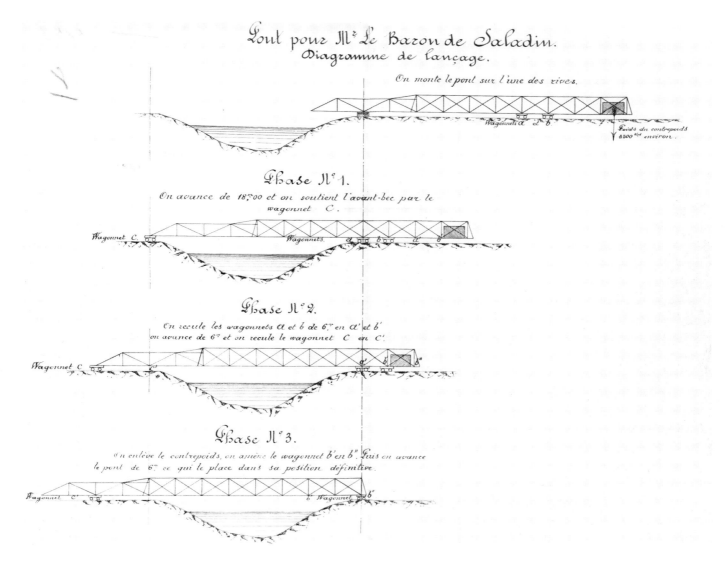

47

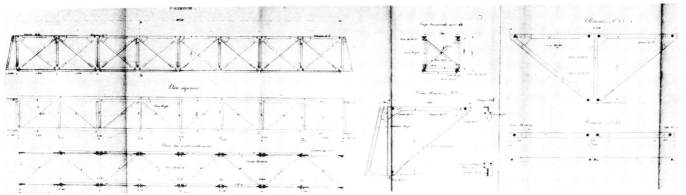

26 *10-meter portable bridges for Upper Senegal*, general view and details, October 1883, print, Paris, Archives nationales.

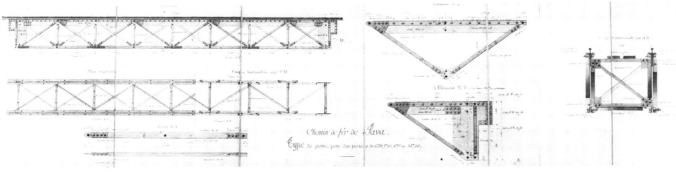

27 *Bridge for the Java railroad*, elevation, details, cross section, pen and watercolor, Paris, Archives nationales.

28 *Eiffel system bridge*, location unknown, photograph, Paris, Musée d'Orsay, Eiffel collection.

29   Eiffel system demountable bridge for normal gauge (1.50 meter) railroad, type for spans of less than 45 meters, photograph, Paris, Musée d'Orsay, Eiffel collection.

30   *Eiffel Bridge, Dijon*, view taken on September 16, 1907, photograph, Paris, Musée d'Orsay, Eiffel collection.

31 *Bridge over the Roubion, Montélimar*, steel bowstring, June 10, 1887, photograph, Paris, Musée d'Orsay, Eiffel collection.

32 *Bridge over the Roubion, Montélimar*, steel bowstring, June 10, 1887, photograph, Paris, Musée d'Orsay, Eiffel collection.

33 *Bridge over the Rach-Lang* (district of Saigon), 1885.   34 *Bridge at Dong-Nhyen, near Phu-Tho* (district of Saigon).

35   *Bascule bridge over the arroyo de la Poste at Tan An* (Cochin China), May 1890.

36   *Bridge of Santa Cruz de la Laguna, Manila*, February 1891.

over the bridge you delivered to me last year; it stood up to this load perfectly, and I was therefore pleased to note that it was adequate for my requirements. I let twelve oxen weighing 700 kilograms each cross over it at liberty, and the bridge did not even bend. I therefore declare that after all the experiments I have been able to carry out, although I could not reach a weight of 4 tonnes, the bridge you delivered to me is quite sufficient for the use to which it is put."[9] The Baron Saladin, who had a 24-meter-span bridge on his estate at Bossancourt, in the Aube department, expressed the same satisfaction: "I have always been perfectly satisfied with the bridge, over which 120,000 pounds of hay and several wagons heavily loaded with building stone have passed. In addition, it is constantly used by carriages. Everyone compliments me on its strength, which does not prevent its having a very lightweight appearance." At Eiffel's request, he had a 4-tonne single-axled cart cross over the bridge in the presence of the regional representative of the Highways Department, and it was established that the maximum bending was 18 millimeters.[10]

Saladin, Clayeux, or the Vicomte Decazes, who was contemplating a bridge across the Vienne River, to link his land at Villars to the village of

37 Marcellin Varcollier, *Interior of the Synagogue in the Rue des Tourelles,* watercolor, private collection.

Gouex,[11] are good examples of those "modern" farming landowners who were always on the lookout for the latest technological novelty. Nevertheless, most of Eiffel's custom still came from the administration: the Naval Ministry placed bridges in Upper Senegal (for the Upper Senegal railroad), in Tonkin (during the Tonkin Expedition), and in Martinique (a bridge over the river Pilote); the War Ministry placed them at Versailles, in Tonkin, and in the Lower Alps; and the local administration of Cochin-China introduced them all over the country; and there were also orders from foreign governments in Belgium, Romania, Russia, and Italy.

Although these portable bridges made up the everyday work of the Levallois-Perret workshops, and enabled the firm to carry on smoothly, it is for his great constructions that Eiffel's name should be remembered. However, the company's early days were not easy. There were a few jobs here and there, such as the outer metal structure of the synagogue built in the Rue des Tournelles by Marcellin Varcollier, a job paying 180,000 francs which was financed by the City of Paris: "You see that I take all kinds of custom," Eiffel commented to his father.[12] There was also the construction of forty-two little bridges on the Poitiers-Limoges railroad line ("The remuneration is not high, but I hope to manage by taking great care in the manufacture"),[13] and that of the gasworks at Versailles, Boulogne, Vaugirard, and Passy. Up until the mid-1870s, when he won the contract for the Douro bridge, business was nevertheless uneven. Although Eiffel was unruffled, during a general economic slump in 1866, when many workshops were idle, and in 1869, after an important contract for metal lighthouses in Egypt had fallen through as a result of "influence and bribery,"[14] his tone was decidedly pessimistic. "There are a few contracts which I shall try to win, but they can only be at very low fees."[15] The war and the Commune did nothing to help matters. At Levallois they were living "literally in the midst of the din from mitrailleuses, calls to arms, etc., not to mention the spectacle of events occurring every day in the street."[16] With the suppression of the Commune (Eiffel was particularly delighted that society would be rid of those "filthy rogues"[17] for a long time to come), the closing of the city gates prevented him from reaching his workshops. By December the situation had hardly improved: "Some contracts which I have

FIG. 1. — VIADUC DE LA SIOULE.

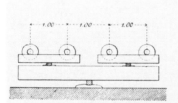

FIG. 2. — CHASSIS DE LANÇAGE
A BASCULE A 4 GALETS.

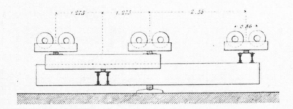

FIG. 3. — CHASSIS DE LANÇAGE A BASCULE.
A 6 PAIRES DE GALETS.

FIG 4 ET 5. — VIADUC DE LA TARDES.

38 *Viaducts of la Sioule and la Tardes*, details of the launching gear, plate from the *Biographie industrielle et scientifique*, vol. 1, Paris, Musée d'Orsay, Eiffel collection.

pending are taking a long time to come through, and this, combined with the transport problems, means that work is a little sluggish."[18] It was only in the spring of 1875, with the contract for the Pest station, and a little later that for the Douro bridge, that the company's affairs would really take off.

First Important Commissions

In June 1867, Eiffel won his first big order. In 1863, the Orléans Company had obtained the concession for the line from Commentry to Gannat, near Vichy, in the Allier department, a small section of the east-west line between Lyons and Bordeaux, in a wild, hilly region where tunnels and viaducts could not be avoided. After consultation, they called in Eiffel to construct two viaducts. This appointment, which he owed largely to the support of Wilhelm Nordling, the chief engineer in charge of this work whom he had met through Léon Courras, the general secretary of the central network of the Orléans Company, was very important for the young engineer and businessman. To begin with, it gained him acceptance among the large metal construction companies, since he was invited to tender together with Cail, Gouin, and Schneider; moreover, the contract brought his young firm large sums of money which would, he calculated, guarantee him eighteen months' security. He therefore wrote proudly to his mother on June 8, 1867: "This morning I saw the engineers' report on the project, and it concludes that my plans are so satisfactory that on the one hand I have been given the contract for part of the work, and on the other, the Cail Company, which is undertaking the rest, is to execute the work according to my plans. I have about 550,000 francs' worth of work. This is therefore a double success for me, first for my pride and second for the importance of the work which is exactly the type to put me among the companies to be reckoned with."[19] The other two viaducts, over the Bouble and the Bellon, which were of the same type but longer (395 meters and 231 meters respectively), were granted to Cail in association with Fives-Lille. For the part of the work which he had

39 *Viaduct of la Sioule,* 1869, photograph, Paris, Musée d'Orsay, Eiffel collection.

been granted, the viaducts at Rouzat on the Sioule (180 meters, finished in the fall of 1869) and at Neuvial (160 meters, completed at the end of 1868), Eiffel took up Nordling's plans, as he had been instructed to do, but made substantial improvements on them. In fact, the columns of the piers in the viaducts designed by Nordling—that on the Sarine River near Fribourg, for example—were of cast iron, which prevented rust, but made for less reliable jointing with the wrought-iron components of the bracing than wrought iron would have, since the parts were held together merely by bolts instead of rivets. To counteract this weakness, Eiffel decided to use joints similar to wrought-iron ones, with riveted gusset plates. To this end, he

proposed that the gusset plates be made with communicating spaces to ensure jointing by means of lugs which would be incorporated into the cast-iron part, and that they should be inserted during casting by suspending them in the mold. This method successfully produced perfect jointing "without voids or gas pores."[20]

Another of Eiffel's innovations was the improvement of the method of rolling out. Rolling out, as he himself noted, is "the operation whereby a deck previously assembled on the embankment is rolled out into space until it meets the successive piers."[21] This process, which had been introduced during construction of the Sioule viaduct in 1869 and was employed through construction of the Tardes viaduct in 1883, was widely used. Eiffel, who had adopted "the lever method, which involves directly activating the rollers on which the bridge is resting, so as to avoid any tendency of the piers to overturn

40   *Church of San Marcos, Arica, Chile,* façade.

during the gradual movement, [...] devised bascule frames designed to hold these rollers, which subsequently became widely adopted. These devices, because they can move around a horizontal axis, distribute stress from the deck evenly over all the rollers, so that no part of the girder bears a load greater than that calculated. This arrangement, shown in Figure 2, is very important because the lower part of the girders is not horizontal, and because by using bascule frames, the rollers are supported on the steps formed by the different thicknesses of sheet metal on which the rolling takes place."[22]

Although it was not until 1875, with the contracts for the station at Pest and the Douro bridge, that Eiffel's firm attained international stature, the years 1869–75 were not without activity, despite Eiffel's complaints and France's economic difficul-

ties after a costly war and revolution. There were bridges on the line from Brive to Tulle (1870), bridges on the Tours-Les Sables-d'Olonne line, and the casino at Les Sables-d'Olonne. But the company began to become especially involved in construction abroad during those years: in Central Europe (bridges on the line from Jassy to Ungheni in Romania, 1872), in Egypt (the Salemleck footbridge, 1873), in the Far East (the metal framework of the church in Manila, in the Philippines, in 1875), and, above all, in South America. Eiffel's agent there, Lelièvre, enjoyed his complete confidence, and business boomed: the Arica customs house and pier in Chile (1872), the La Paz gasworks in Bolivia, the Oroya railroad bridges in Peru, as well as the San Marcos church in Arica, which was made entirely of metal and was sent from Levallois-Perret in separate parts and assembled on site. But when Lelièvre died he was not replaced, and commissions in South America became less frequent.

41 *Church of San Marcos, Arica, Chile,* interior.

Budapest Station

In 1875, Eiffel won two important contracts almost simultaneously: the station at Pest in Hungary and the bridge over the Douro in Portugal, which would be by far the largest commissions he had dealt with up until then. In 1874, the Austrian State Railroad Company, which controlled the Vienna–Budapest line as part of its vast network, decided to replace the terminus station which had been built about twenty years before, and which had become completely inadequate. The Austro-Hungarian government wanted a grandiose, monumental station, one that was worthy of the Hungarian capital. The specifications clearly defined the layout of the principal building; the construction manager, de Serres, had in fact laid down, with the aid of plans and sections, the general conditions which the construction had to satisfy, "while allowing the candidates a fairly broad scope for the elaboration of the details." The controlling idea, expressed for the first time in a structure of this type and size, "was that the buildings should consist of a metal framework filled in with ashlar for the base and facing brickwork for the upper walls."[23]

At the beginning of April 1875, the proposal presented by Eiffel and Company, which showed a substantial saving on the rival tenders, was adopted. "It is a 2,700,000 franc contract to be carried out over two years," Eiffel wrote his mother on April 7, "and I am sure it will be profitable. I have already subcontracted the parts of the work which would cause me most problems, such as the masonry and joinery, on good terms. All in all it is a contract which gives me the best possible conditions in terms of fee, profits, and security, and in terms of the future."[24] The work, begun in September 1875, was finished exactly two years later. It was unusual in that the old station, which was much smaller, was largely contained within the metal nave of the new one, so that service was not disturbed in the least during construction; a short time before opening, the old buildings were quickly demolished.

In his *Biographie industrielle et scientifique*, Eiffel gives a brief sketch of the realization of the work. "This station, which is quite decorative and very beautifully constructed, and which covers an area of 13,000 meters, is particularly interesting because it represents one of the first combined uses of metal and masonry, and because the ornamentation is mainly formed by the metal parts of the structure which are left visible."[25] This was indeed the first time that the great nave with its two-leaved, glass-paneled roof covering the platforms had been made so visible from the outside. There is an unfortunate heaviness and banality about the adjoining blocks, which house the administrative offices, and which Eiffel considered full of "originality and elegance." They contrive to be rococo, Moorish, and Renaissance all at once (which is still quite an achievement), but they nevertheless take nothing away from the elegance of the glass-paneled gable, with its projecting canopy supported on coupled columns. The frankness of this approach, at a time when so many of the stations being constructed were hiding their metal framework in a covering of masonry, deserves to be stressed. "In the elevation drawings," Eiffel commented, "we tried to accentuate the main lines of construction through the continuous line of the cornices and string courses, and [...] while retaining the particular character given to the façade from the start, we sought to capture the clarity and simplicity of composition which a building of this type should show [...] We have carefully brought out the role and the nature of the various materials used as clearly as possible."[26]

Thus, despite the inevitable compromises—iron and glass could not be monumental, so the façade had to be of stone and brick—there is in the Pest station a concern for architectural integrity which was all too rare at that time. When Eiffel presented this work at the Universal Exhibition in 1878 with the aid of a perspective drawing and an album of photographs, the tone he took was already that of his reply to the future critics of the 300-meter tower: the intention of a building should be openly declared; the various materials should be used in a deliberate way; why should the industrial nature of a building be disguised, even in the middle of a city?[27]

42 *Pest Station*, perspective view, plate from the *Biographie industrielle et scientifique*, vol. 1, Paris, Musée d'Orsay, Eiffel collection.

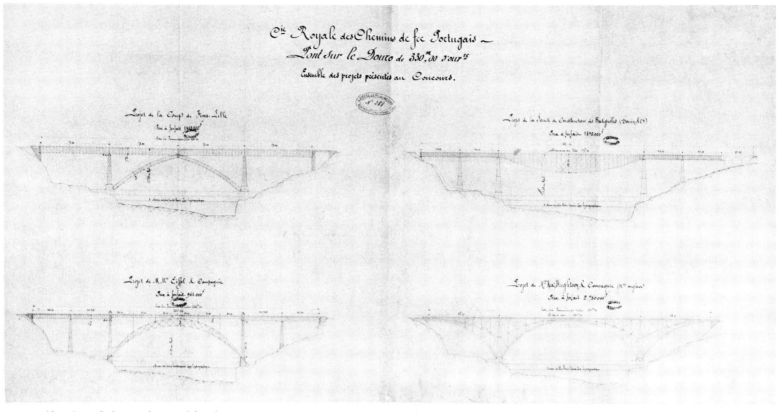

43 *Set of plans submitted for the Douro Bridge competition* (top left, Fives-Lille plan; bottom left, Eiffel plan; top right, plan by the Batignolles Construction Co.; bottom right, Mead, Wrightson & Co.'s plan), pencil, Paris, Archives nationales.

44 *Douro Bridge; design by Mead, Wrightson & Co.*, plan and elevation, pen and watercolor, Paris, Archives nationales.

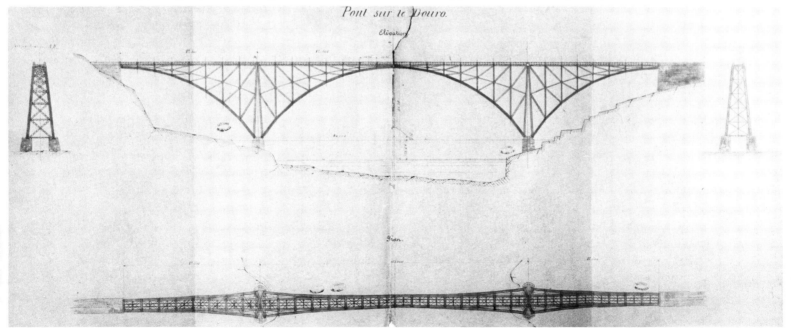

The Douro Bridge

The second big order of 1875 was the bridge over the Douro, which, together with the Garabit viaduct, is still today the most famous of the bridges built by Gustave Eiffel. In 1875, the Royal Portuguese Railroad Company had organized a competition for the bridge which was to cross the river Douro, on the line between Lisbon and Oporto. The difficulties were numerous: the depth of the water, which was as high as 20 meters; the frequency and extent of flooding; the "soil, which was liable to cave in, being formed from a layer of gravel so deep that its thickness could not be established by sounding, and the very rapid currents"[28] made it impossible for piers to be constructed in the river, with the result that the piers nearest the center had to stand on either bank of the river; this meant that the central clear span would be 160 meters long. The largest spans then existing, excluding suspension bridges, were those of the Britannia bridge (140 meters), the Kuilenbourg bridge (150 meters), and the Saint Louis bridge over the Mississippi (158.50 meters).

On May 1, 1875, four schemes, all original and carefully designed, were submitted. In the paper he presented to the Société des Ingénieurs Civils in 1875, Théophile Seyrig described them in detail[29]; a drawing preserved in the French National Archives enables us to attribute them to their respective designers.[30] The first one, which used "the general form of a crane with two jibs" was that of the English firm Mead, Wrightson, and Company; it consisted of "a great semicircular central arch resting on abutments placed at the edge of the river. The two trussed girders forming this arch rested on separate masonry blocks, thus making four in all. Other half-arches rested on these supports, with their apexes, supported by the abutments, forming the ends of the bridge." This was a prophetic project, since, as Gilbert Cordier noted, it pointed forward to the scheme which was to be used thirty years later for the Viaur viaduct built by the Société de Construction des Batignolles in 1896.[31]

In its sketch for the Douro bridge, the Batignolles Construction Company itself proposed a solution which made use of "two principal masonry abutment piers placed on the riverbank, supporting a girder with a span of 170 meters. The girder was semiparabolic in form, and its height at the center was 22.50 meters. The principal trussed girders were to be of steel. The single track rested on the upper part."[32]

The Fives-Lille Company's proposal, which foreshadowed Maillart's propped bridges, formed the structure "by means of four equal spans of 78 meters each. Two metal piers were placed at the edge of the river. The third support needed for these four spans was formed in the middle of the river by two great curved raking props, resting on the same masonry foundations as the piers."

Finally, the Eiffel Company's proposal, which Seyrig saved until last in his paper, would cross the river "by means of a large central arch of unusual shape supporting at five points a straight deck of a length corresponding to its span. The flanking parts of the deck were divided into spans of 43 and 45 meters each, and rested on metal piers."[33]

One thing which immediately separated the competitors out was the marked difference in their estimates: from 1,410,000 francs for the bridge proposed by the Fives-Lille Company to 1,895,000 francs for that of the Batignolles Construction Company (Gouin & Co.), and up to 2,760,000 francs for the Mead, Wrightson, and Company's proposal. The price proposed by Eiffel & Co. as per contract was only 965,000 francs; under these conditions the Portuguese authorities did not hesitate. But before choosing this young company which was still nowhere near as experienced as its rivals, they nevertheless wished to cover themselves with guarantees, and they appointed a commission consisting of people whom Eiffel had known for a long time: Krantz, Molinos, and de Dion. A vitally important contract was at stake for the young businessman. "It is a large bridge," he wrote his mother on May 17, "for which I have submitted the best proposal, with better terms than Fives-Lille, Gouin, and an English firm. It would be one of the biggest bridges in Europe. If I win the contract, I shall certainly be established as one of the major construction firms."[34]

As it turned out, the commission's opinion was favorable, and Eiffel's proposal was carried out "almost exactly as it had been designed." Begun in January 1876, the work on the "masonry, the piers, and the straight decks" was completed by September. The winter floods made further progress impossible, and it was only in March 1877 that assembly of the arch could begin; on October 31

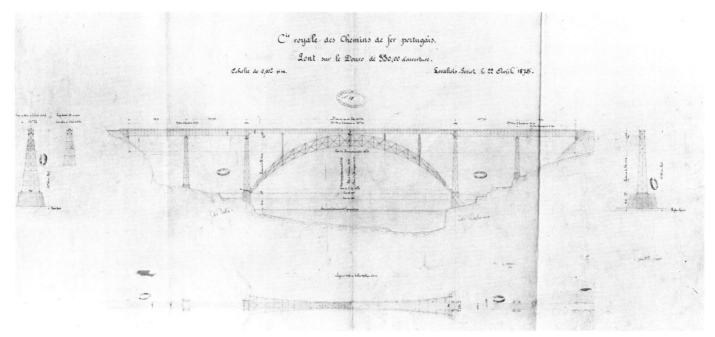

45   *Douro Bridge; Eiffel's design*, plan and elevation, April 1875, pencil, Paris, Archives nationales.

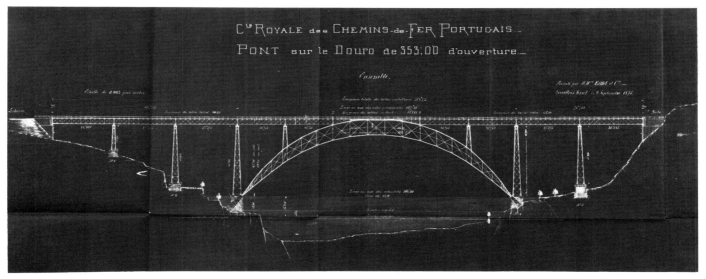

46   *Douro Bridge; Eiffel's design*, elevation, blueprint, September 1875, Paris, Archives nationales.

the bridge was finished, and on November 4 it was ceremonially opened "amid a great crowd of people" by King Luis I of Portugal and Queen Maria-Pia, after whom the bridge was named.[35]

As in the case of the 300-meter tower, it is difficult to define exactly the part played by Gustave Eiffel in the entirely new design of this structure, which was subsequently used for the Garabit viaduct. In the account he wrote of it for the Universal Exhibition of 1878—he showed a 1/50th scale model of it in Class 66 (Civil Engineering)—Eiffel mentioned the names of two collaborators in "working out the calculations and drawing up the project," Théophile Seyrig and Henry de Dion.[36] In 1878, Seyrig presented the paper from which we have already quoted to the Société des Ingénieurs

Civils. The following year Eiffel, who had no wish to be left out, and had not appreciated his partner's attitude, published a *Notice sur le pont du Douro à Porto*, which indisputably established his authorship of the project, or so he thought. These were recurrent quarrels which were to accompany all Eiffel's major constructions, including both the Garabit viaduct and the tower.

Although Eiffel would systematically suppress Théophile Seyrig's name later on, he was more just towards Henry de Dion, whose name was inscribed with those of seventy-one other scientists on the outside frieze of the first level of the tower in 1889. De Dion, who was four years older than Eiffel, had died eleven years previously on April 13, 1878; but at the time of the Universal Exhibition of 1889, his old discoveries were still innovative, since the daring and elegant roof trusses without tie beams used in the Galerie des Machines were his work.

The report de Dion presented at the request of the Portuguese Railroad Company on June 30, 1875 dwelt on Eiffel's project, praising its novelty and its very prudent boldness. He concluded the report as follows: "The complete study of a structure of this size presents great difficulties. The methods of calculation known up to now can only be applied in practice with the aid of hypotheses which depart from established facts to a greater or lesser extent, and thus render the projected results uncertain."[37]

In the final analysis only experience could prove the accuracy of the Eiffel Company's hypotheses. Eiffel, who, as all his contemporaries noted, was a remarkable construction site manager and leader of men, went to Portugal himself with his wife, and stayed in a house in the country near Oporto. From the *Mémoire présenté à l'appui du projet* (now in the National Archives in Paris) to the opening of the bridge two years later, only minor details were changed. Eiffel used the description given in the *Mémoire* to accompany the model shown at the Universal Exhibition in 1878.

With a total length of 352.75 meters, and a maximum height of 62.40 meters, "this great structure consists of a central span over the course of the Douro itself, joined to the top of the valley by a viaduct at either end."[38] We have noted the natural obstacles which prevented the piers being built in the course of the river itself, and the consequent need to construct a single arch with its supports resting on the rocks level with each of the banks. "Because of the great height available for use, we decided to build this part in the form of an arch on which the horizontal deck carrying the track rests. This straight-girder deck is supported by metal piers whose height varies according to the configuration of the ground."[39]

The dimensions of the arch required arrangements for which the calculations were hazardous, as the commission examining the project emphasized: "Above all it was absolutely necessary to dispense with the use of rigid spandrels. The calculation for these, which is very uncertain, would be rendered even more complicated by the effects of expansion, which would considerably

47   *Douro Bridge; diagram of the different phases of assembly,* print, Paris, Archives nationales.

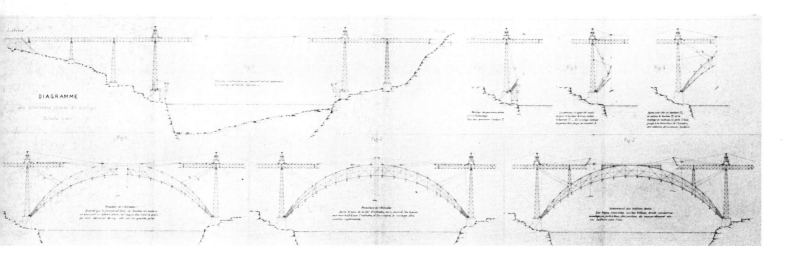

48 *Douro Bridge*, detail of metal pier, blueprint, Paris, Archives nationales.

49 *Douro Bridge*, detail of abutment pier, pen and watercolor, Paris, Archives nationales.

50–52 *Assembly of the Douro* ▷ *Bridge, Oporto*, photographs, Paris, Musée d'Orsay, Eiffel collection.

upset the balance of the different components of which the spandrels would be made. Thus we would have had to use a large amount of metal which would still not have ensured adequate safety. It therefore seemed preferable in every respect to do away with the spandrels completely by making the truss itself sufficiently rigid to withstand the deforming stresses resulting from the unequal distribution of loads. We did this by making the truss very deep; at the apex its depth is 10 meters."[40]

Another problem was that of wind resistance. "So that it could resist the violence of storms, it had to be very wide at the base, or at least have a large footing at the base, for it was pointless to make the upper part any wider than was needed to carry the track, that is, approximately 4.00 meters." The

metal part of the structure therefore consisted of the following parts:

1) A metal arch with a span of 160 meters, and a rise of 42.60 meters measured at the neutral axis, carrying two metal bents 22.25 meters from the springing of the arch;

2) A central deck integral with the arch, 51.88 meters long;

3) A flanking deck on the Lisbon side, 169.87 meters long, resting on the one hand on the arch and the bent which is fixed to the extrados, and on the other hand on two intermediary metal piers and the abutment on the Lisbon side. It is divided into two spans of 28.75 meters for the part above the arch and three spans of 37.375 meters for the part above the bank.

4) A flanking deck on the Oporto side, 132.50 meters long, and resting, like the first, both on the arch and the bent fixed to the extrados, and on the two metal piers and the abutment. Thus it consists of four spans, two of 28.75 meters, and two of 37.375 meters.[41]

The final innovation in this decidedly unusual bridge was the method of erection. Eiffel was able to rely on the assistance of three of his collaborators: Emile Nouguier, Joseph Collin, and Angevère. The latter two played only a minor role (as we have noted, Collin was Eiffel's brother-in-law, and was soon dismissed for unremitting inefficiency). Nouguier, whom his employer unjustly placed on the same level as the other two, is well known to us thanks to the account devoted to him in Georges Barral's *Panthéon scientifique de la Tour Eiffel*.[42] Born in Paris in 1840, a graduate engineer of the Ecole Nationale Supérieure des Mines, he was employed by the Batignolles Construction Company (Ernest Gouin's company) from 1867 to 1876, first as head of the drawing office and then as site

engineer; so he was working for this company when they tendered for the Douro bridge. In 1876, he started work for Eiffel as engineer in charge of supervising technical drawings and assembly, and he left immediately for Portugal, where he actively supervised the construction of this great structure, as he would later the work at Garabit. The nature of the terrain made any falsework impossible; the arches were therefore built out from the springing on each side, and were "supported, as construction progressed, by steel cables which were fixed to the upper deck. Each of the sections constructed acted as a support for the erection of the following sections. By this gradual process, the two parts of the truss moved towards one another and came out to meet in space, where the key which would join them was to be put in position."[43] This difficult and original operation, whose mathematical progression can be seen from photographs, was conducted with masterly precision by Eiffel; when the two sections of the truss met at the center, thanks to the strict work in the workshop and the accuracy of the assembly, the horizontal deviation between them was only about one centimeter. In the vertical plane a greater margin had been provided for. "The elasticity of the cables, the bending of the arch while it was being cantilevered, the variations in temperature, and other considerations made it

53   *Perspective view of the Douro Bridge, Oporto*, engraving, Paris, Musée d'Orsay, Eiffel collection.

desirable to have a certain margin available at the moment when the two sections met, so that they would be finally joined by lowering them one towards the other. The cable moorings were arranged so that the cables could be lowered gradually, to assemble the last joint. This operation was performed slowly but smoothly and easily. The end of the arch was lowered by about 350 millimeters."[44]

It was Seyrig who was to define the importance of the Douro bridge most clearly, stressing the intrinsic beauty of the structure which made no "architectural" concessions and owed everything to the art of the engineer. Eiffel was to take the same tone when he defended his tower fifteen years later. It was not true that metal construction systematically neglected the "study of form"; a metal bridge "does not spoil the landscape," and "does not obstruct the view of the entrancing countryside in which it is situated in any way." "The arch form," Seyrig continues, "has always been considered the most elegant [...]. Its construction, using a small number of large elements, gives the impression of robustness and power, while the whole retains the lightness imparted to it by the use of metal."[45]

The debates over the intrusion of industrial construction into a "respectable," almost sacrosanct place, would recur when the great metal tower was being erected with mathematical precision in the Paris of the 1880s. Like the Garabit viaduct, the Douro bridge has an algebraic beauty, a clarity and simplicity of form which make it one of the finest works of the nineteenth century. Eiffel was certainly aware of this, but, more pragmatic than Seyrig, and realizing all that this brilliant success could bring to his young company in the way of business, he concluded more drily: "The boldness of the method, and the size of the span, which was greater than that of any bridge constructed up to then (apart from suspension bridges), focused the attention of informed people all over the world on the name of Monsieur Eiffel."[46]

Expansion of the Company in France and Throughout the World

From the Douro bridge until the construction of the tower, the Eiffel Company's order book was never empty. The articles of the new Compagnie des Etablissements Eiffel in 1890 gave a statement of circumstances and emphasized that business was good.[47] The company had offices in Saigon, Shanghai, and Lisbon, not to mention the commission agents in St. Petersburg, Buenos Aires, Madrid, and Naples; it possessed thirteen patents in France and seven abroad, for the most varied of items: "for a new arrangement for the deck of bridges, with a view to facilitating navigation" (1876); "for a hydrostatic uplift observation dome system" (1881); "for a new arrangement enabling the construction of metal piers and pylons higher than 300 meters" (1885); "for a continuous-circuit suspended aerial railroad system, to be used to transport visitors at an exhibition" (1886). It would be tedious to list everything that Gustave Eiffel's company was constructing at that time in the world. The work on the Pest station and the Douro bridge had made it more stable than it had ever been before. The Universal Exhibition of 1878 established it definitively as one of the major French metal construction companies. Not only did Eiffel exhibit "machines, models, and drawings" showing his main constructions—"the Maria-Pia bridge over the Douro, a road bridge planned for the port of Oporto, a road and rail bridge at Vianna do Castello (Portugal), the principal building of the new Buda-Pest station (Hungary)"—but he also carried out considerable work for the exhibition itself.

The Universal Exhibition of 1878 was hastily decided upon two years earlier by the young French republic to prove not only the virtues and capabilities of the new regime, but also to show that France, which had suffered war, revolution, and the amputation of part of its territory, was rapidly rising again from its ashes; as such, the exhibition, rather than an architectural display, was primarily an expression of political will. "By announcing the new International Exhibition to the world, France is affirming her confidence in the institutions she has set up for herself; she is declaring her will to pursue the ideas of moderation and steadiness which have inspired her policies for the last five years. She is proclaiming that she wants peace, the only thing which has the power to make human activity truly fertile, by giving it security."[48] Such were the declarations about which Eiffel probably cared very little; he paid attention only to the healthy state of business and (as we saw in his diatribe against the Communards) the stability of

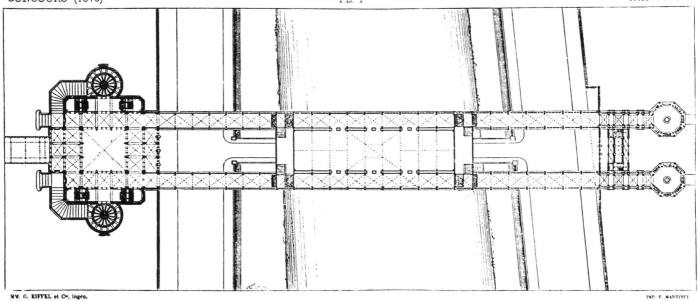

MM. G. EIFFEL et Cⁱᵉ, ingén.　　　　　　　　　　　　　　　　　IMP. F. MARTINET

EXPOSITION UNIVERSELLE DE PARIS EN 1878

PASSAGE AU-DESSUS DU PONT D'IÉNA

54　*Gallery above the Iéna Bridge*, plan, 1876 competition for the 1878 Universal Exhibition, plate from the *Encyclopédie d'Architecture*, September 1876.

55　*Gallery above the Iéna Bridge*, cross section and elevation, 1876 competition for the 1878 Universal Exhibition, plate from the *Encyclopédie d'Architecture*, September 1876.

ENCYCLOPÉDIE D'ARCHITECTURE

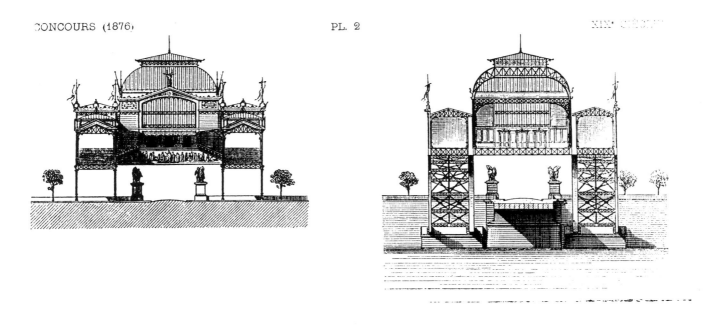

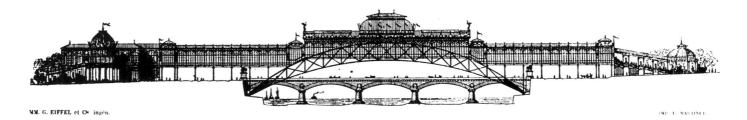

MM. G. EIFFEL et Cⁱᵉ ingén.　　　　　　　　　　　　　　　　　IMP. F. MARTINET

EXPOSITION UNIVERSELLE DE PARIS EN 1878

PASSAGE AU-DESSUS DU PONT D'IÉNA

the government. When construction was going well, everything was as it should be.

The general commissioner for the exhibition was Jean-Baptiste Krantz, who had designed the palace for 1867 with Le Play, and for whom Eiffel had already worked. Various competitions were launched, notably one for a covered bridge connecting the Champ de Mars to the Trocadero gardens. Whereas the 1855 Exhibition had consisted merely of a few isolated buildings (the Palais de l'Industrie on the Champs-Elysées, the Galerie des Machines along the Seine, the Palais des Beaux-Arts on the Avenue Montaigne), that of 1867 had already filled the whole of the Champ de Mars, with the main palace surrounded by a vast number of the pavilions which were henceforth to become a characteristic of Universal Exhibitions. By 1878, the Champ de Mars, temporarily cleared by the army, was no longer enough; the exhibition stretched out on the other side of the Seine up to Davioud and Bourdais's Trocadero Palace which had been designed to hold a large hall, and which crowned the Chaillot hill. One of the main problems facing the organizers was that of constructing links between the buildings, which became more and more scattered. So that visitors should not feel a break between the two banks, continuity was

needed between the two sides of the Seine (as would be the case again in 1900, and with the abortive 1909 Exhibition).

In 1878, the competition program therefore stipulated a covered bridge linking the buildings on the Champ de Mars to those of the Trocadero, passing above the Iéna bridge, "high enough to allow traffic to circulate freely on the bridge and the embankments. Moreover, it should carry a closed gallery to shelter visitors going from one bank to the other from bad weather, and it should be constructed in such a way that the visitor crossing it is not given the impression of leaving one exhibition and going into another."[49]

Thus the bridge had to be an original and attractive exhibition building, and not merely a utilitarian footbridge. Going back to the "rigid arch system" which had just been tried out on the Douro bridge, Eiffel proposed "that the deck of the bridge be supported by a single arch with a span of 150 meters, consisting of rigid trusses, and having no intermediary support in the river."[50] In fact, this

56 Léopold Hardy, *Main façade of the Palais du Champ de Mars*, 1878 Universal Exhibition.

would mean exhibiting for a limited time in the very heart of Paris the young contractor's boldest and most successful work, disguised as exhibition architecture. Eiffel easily found arguments in favor of adopting this system: "In this case, it seemed advantageous to use our type of bridge to cross the Seine. This does away with the necessity of supporting it on the Iéna bridge, whose foundations might not have borne the extra load without danger, and moreover, it would not use supports in the river, as any other system would necessarily do, thus avoiding further obstacles to navigation at a point where there will be an exceptional amount of traffic which will certainly be hampered by the narrowness of the arches of the Iéna bridge."[51]

Eiffel's final argument, which was particularly convincing when backed up by the elevation draw-ing of the bridge, was that nothing could demonstrate more clearly the progress which had been made over a few years in the art of bridge building than the juxtaposition of the rather ordinary Iéna bridge (1809–13), with its five masonry arches, and the airy metal footbridge.

The cost of the structure, some 2,780,000 francs according to the estimate presented by Eiffel (compared with 965,000 francs for the Douro bridge!), and its unavoidable height which concealed most of the constructions on the Trocadero from the Champ de Mars, meant that Eiffel's proposal, like those of his rivals, was unsuccessful. However, his participation in the Universal Exhibition of 1878 was not limited to this abortive project. In fact, Messieurs G. Eiffel and Company, under the direction of Duval, the chief engineer and Director of Works, erected "very considerable"[52] metal structures, including the Great Iéna Entrance Hall, the City of Paris Exhibition Pavilion, and the more modest exhibition pavilion of the Paris Gas Company.

57   J.A. Bouvard, *Pavilion of the City of Paris,* 1878 Universal Exhibition.

What was then known as the Great Iéna Entrance Hall extended along the main façade of the Palais du Champ de Mars designed by Léopold Hardy. In 1867, the exhibition hall had been in the form of an ellipse; in 1878, it was to be rectangular, 700 meters long by 300 meters wide, a series of parallel metal halls with a Gallery of Machines at either side. The entrance hall on the side facing the Trocadero, which had been entrusted to Eiffel, was 300 meters long by 26 meters wide, punctuated by three domes, one at the center and one at each end. "The end domes are in plan 35-meter squares. From the ground to the bottom of the lightning conductor they are 45 meters high. The central dome covers a space 40 meters by 33 meters. It is not as high as the end domes—only 35 meters high; it is in the form of the segment of a sphere with a diameter of 30 meters, resting on four iron columns. Two extensions forming elliptical scallops on the inside have been placed on the sides, which face onto the end domes, so as to connect the main sphere to the wings of the entrance hall. The straight parts on either side of the central dome are formed from eleven roof trusses 10 meters apart, supporting a pitched roof which is 19.50 meters high at the ridge. These trusses, which are a continuation of the columns, have no tie beams and thus it is through their own stiffness that they resist the thrust."[53]

In 1878, the partisans of iron were victorious. Thanks to de Dion, who died without seeing his work complete, the great roof trusses without tie beams made it possible to do away with all intermediary supports in the Gallery of Machines; in the *Encyclopédie d'Architecture*, Charles Blanc declared, a little hastily, that henceforth nothing would distinguish the engineer from the architect.[54] His enthusiasm was not shared by all. The same journal considered the metal domes questionable, calling them "great skeletons enclosing objects which in no way call for shelters of such gigantic proportions."[55] The supporters of "iron and nothing but iron" criticized the inevitable decorative exterior, the heaviness and unjustifiably large size of the whole; and it was true that Hardy's palace, heterogeneous, tentative, and badly arranged, did not leave much of a memory. Eiffel could do nothing about this, but he won little praise for this brief collaboration.

More interesting was the City of Paris Pavilion, a "large rectangular hall 80 meters long by 25 me-ters wide" designed by Bouvard, the city architect, and by Henry de Dion, the exhibition engineer for metal structures, "with the collaboration of Messieurs Eiffel and Company."[56] As Eiffel noted, this was a fine example of "the application of terracotta and enamels to wrought and cast iron."[57] It was to house the models of recent works by the City of Paris. In the center was the triumphant model of the new city hall by Ballu and Deperthes, reconstructed "exactly the same" after having been burned down in the Commune, which would be opened four years later. There were also models of Lheureux's law faculty, La Villette's markets and abattoirs, and the civic halls of the eleventh, fifteenth, and nineteenth arrondissements, and the "model, plan, section, and elevation of a part of a street—the houses, the roadways, the boulevards with their benches and kiosks, with every detail perfectly accurate. The section facing the visitors shows the underground pipes which distribute the water and gas necessary for private houses and the public highway. On the right and the left, sections are cut through the houses, so as to show the distribution of water and gas from the basement to the top story, and the drainage system for household water and for the sewers."[58]

To complement this unusual scheme, the architect, and especially the two engineers, covered the vast hall with 3,140 square meters of horizontal glass ceiling; "the roof trusses, which are triangular in section, are 15 meters apart, and rest on wrought-iron pillars embedded in the walls, and on cast-iron columns 2.50 meters in front of these."[59] These columns supported mobile partitions which allowed the space to be divided up as required, served as a background to the models, and could be used for hanging plans and photographs. Handsome and daring, practical, innovative in its use and combination of different materials, this pavilion survived the 1878 Exhibition; it was rebuilt on the other side of the Seine, near the Palais de l'Industrie, and shared its fate, being demolished during the preparations for the Universal Exhibition of 1900.

If we add to these two large-scale works the Paris Gas Company's pavilion, on which Eiffel collaborated for the first time with Stephen Sauvestre, the architect of the tower, the presentation of the iron revolving crane without base, and the work carried out in Portugal and Hungary, the Universal Exhibition of 1878 was a great success for Eiffel,

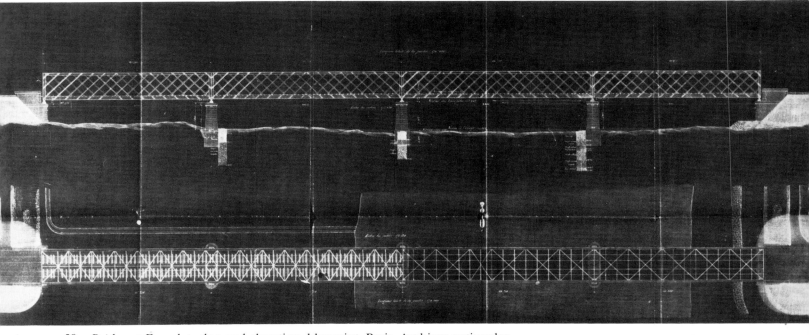

58   *Bridge at Empalot*, plan and elevation, blueprint, Paris, Archives nationales.

59   *Bridge at Varzeas*, Beira-Alta railroad, photograph, Paris, Musée d'Orsay, Eiffel collection.

60   *Bridge at Milijoso*, Beira-Alta railroad, photograph, Paris, Musée d'Orsay, Eiffel collection.

61   *Bridge at Trezoï*, Beira-Alta railroad, photograph, Paris, Musée d'Orsay, Eiffel collection.

62 *Bridge at Mortagua*, Beira-Alta railroad, photograph, Paris, Musée d'Orsay, Eiffel collection.

63 *Bridge at Cris*, Beira-Alta railroad, photograph, Paris, Musée d'Orsay, Eiffel collection.

64 *Bridge at Dao*, Beira-Alta railroad, photograph, Paris, Musée d'Orsay, Eiffel collection.

65 *Bridge at Luzo*, Beira-Alta railroad, photograph, Paris, Musée d'Orsay, Eiffel collection.

and firmly established him. He received the Cross of the Légion d'Honneur, he was among the people most in the public eye, and he knew how to get himself talked about; these public-relations skills, as we might call them today, were not insignificant, and, although they did not put his company among the very first French metal construction companies—it was nearer fifth or sixth—they meant that the engineer and businessman's name began to be heard everywhere.

If 1889 was to be his triumph, the "intervening" Universal Exhibition at Antwerp in 1885 showed, even more clearly than that of 1878, how far his business had expanded. Eiffel had exhibits in three different places: in the Gallery of Machines he had a drawing of the Douro bridge, drawings and photographs of the Garabit viaduct, a photograph of the Szeged road bridge and one of the Tardes viaduct, drawings of bridges built in Cochin-China, a "drawing of the Monumental iron Tower 300 meters high, planned for the Universal Exhibition in 1889," and three drawings of the Nice Observatory dome. In the French colonies' pavilion, he showed photographs of structures in Cochin-China, and also a life-size example of an economical portable bridge with a span of 21.00 meters.[60] Garabit, Szeged, the tower, the Nice Observatory: Eiffel's principal works were still to come.

Gustave Eiffel was so much in his element at this time that his private life is pushed into the background—reduced to the banalities which can be observed about any man whose profession swallows up his family life. Nevertheless, the 1870s saw a series of bereavements, one by one, which affected him deeply: Edouard Régneau died in 1874, his wife Marie Gaudelet-Eiffel three years later after a "brief illness," then his parents in Dijon, to whom he had been writing more and more irregularly, giving news of the children and mentioning a few business matters—nothing particularly important. He had to reorganize his life: his eldest daughter Claire would stay with him, taking the place his wife should have occupied. A few years later this was to be one of the conditions he placed on her marriage. "As all of my children know," he noted in a codicil to his will on October 20, 1906, "since the death of my dear wife, I have insisted on my eldest daughter Claire's remaining with me. This was even a condition I imposed on her marriage, taking on all common

expenses as my responsibility. In this respect my daughter and my son-in-law, Monsieur Salles, have shown feelings of filial devotion which made this life together sweet and trouble-free, and were very precious to me in the days of sadness."[61]

From the success of the bridge over the Douro and the Universal Exhibition of 1878, the Eiffel Company's business multiplied, with the Valentine, Sarrieu, and Empalot railroad bridges on the Toulouse-Bayonne line for the Compagnie du Midi, bridges in Romania, the metal frame for the Au Bon Marché shop, and bridges on the Beira-Alta line in Portugal (which led to the creation of a magnificent album commissioned by the Portuguese Railroad Company).

In addition to these constructions, the years 1879–81 saw three major projects which Eiffel, disregarding those cited above, himself described in detail in his *Biographie industrielle et scientifique:* these were the Garabit viaduct, the Szeged road bridge, and the Evaux viaduct over the Tardes. Although they were less spectacular, the structures ranged along the Beira-Alta line in the upper Douro valley were nevertheless the subject of a three-and-a-half-million-franc contract, thus bringing in more than the Garabit viaduct; but the latter, as Eiffel emphasized, was "the most important structure to be built in France up until that time."[62]

The Garabit Viaduct

The success of the Douro bridge, the perfect precision of the assembly which had focused "the attention of informed people all over the world," explains why Eiffel was called on to construct a viaduct on the line from Marvejols to Neussargues in the Cantal, crossing the deep valley of the Truyère at a height of 122 meters. "To give an idea of this height of 122 meters, we need only say that it is considerably greater than that of the towers of Notre-Dame and the column in the Place Vendôme one on top of the other";[63] a popular engraving showed this strange pile of monuments, and that Eiffel's structure was obviously higher.

The procedure through which Eiffel was allocated the contract was unusual: "At the suggestion of Monsieur Bauby and Monsieur Boyer (the State engineers) the Highways Department Board

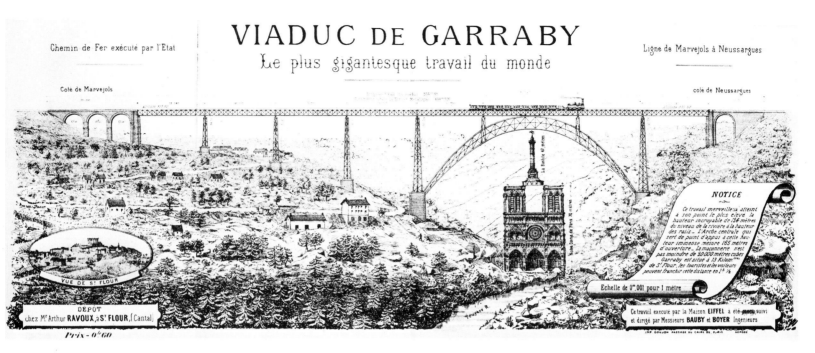

approved the construction of the work on the basis of information about the Douro bridge, and agreed to entrust the construction of both the masonry and the metal part to Monsieur Eiffel, by a private contract."[64] This resolution was the subject of a ministerial decision on June 14, 1879, approving the engineers' initiative, the pilot study which Eiffel had already submitted, his estimate of 1,800,000 francs, and the construction period of eighteen months to two years: "The Engineer in Ordinary considers that the work might be put up for tender, and the major construction firms called on to make proposals and tender for it, but that it would be preferable to deal with Monsieur G. Eiffel, whose proposals appear acceptable to the Engineer, because only Monsieur Eiffel has constructed a similar work, and only he has the experience of the new assembly methods of which he is in large part the inventor, and for which he also has the equipment which was used to erect the bridge over the Douro." Administrative praise could be no higher; the planned competition was put aside. "It would in any case be unjust to entrust the work to any other than Monsieur Eiffel, since it is his Douro bridge which gave the Engineers the idea of crossing the Truyère valley with a new route which should save the State several million francs."[65] A private contract was concluded, and work on the site began in January 1880.

66 *"Viaduct of Garraby, the biggest construction in the world,"* engraving, Paris, Musée d'Orsay, Eiffel collection.

For the building of this structure, Eiffel took on several collaborators whom he listed, as in the case of the Douro bridge, very unobtrusively on the last page of the *Mémoire présenté à l'appui du projet définitif du Viaduc de Garabit,* published in 1889. They were Emile Nouguier, whom we have already met, for the general study of the project and the methods of assembly; Maurice Koechlin for the calculation and drawing up of the project; Jean Compagnon, for the assembly and work on site; and Jean-Baptiste Gobert, Eiffel's assistant in the general direction of the work.

Thus the team which was to build the tower was already formed. The important element in this new "arrangement" was the arrival of Maurice Koechlin as a replacement for Théophile Seyrig, whose legal wrangles with his partner and employer we have already mentioned.[66] Koechlin was born in 1856 in Alsace—he was thus twenty-four when the work began—and had studied at the Polytechnikum in Zurich, where he had finished first in his year. In Paris, he had worked for two years in the technical drawing office of the Eastern Railroads before joining Eiffel's company. Jean Gobert, who was born in 1841 and was thus about ten years younger than Eiffel, was, like him, a graduate of the Ecole Centrale des Arts et Manufactures; he had been working with Eiffel since 1876, after working in Marseilles and Bordeaux, and he had devised "a new theory of the construction of vaults and a graphic method for determining the single thrust line giving the smallest thickness for a keystone and the minimum section for a barrel vault."[67]

Jean Compagnon, by contrast, came from a very different background and had a very different training. He was "a workman who was the son of his works,"[68] as Georges Barral put it wittily. In 1855, at the age of seventeen, he had left his native region (Reyrieux in the Ain department) to come to Paris to see the Universal Exhibition. He had been employed by various framework contractors and had attended night school classes at the Conservatoire des Arts et Métiers, had then worked in Russia on the St. Petersburg-Warsaw line, then in Spain, in Italy, in Russia again, and in Hungary. Eiffel had taken him on for the Douro bridge; subsequently he would work on the construction of the Empalot, Sarrieu, and Valentine bridges over the

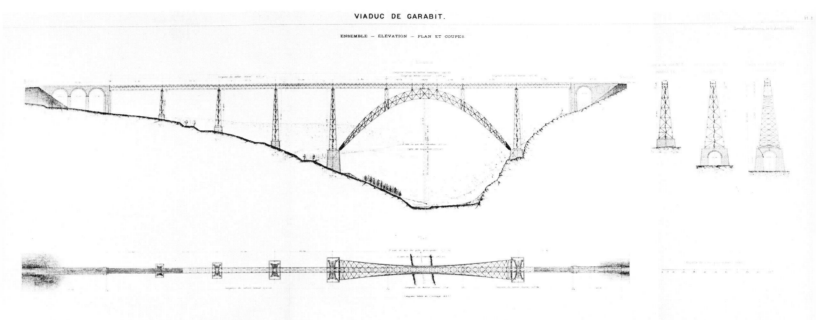

VIADUC DE GARABIT.

ENSEMBLE — ELÉVATION — PLAN ET COUPES

67 *Garabit Viaduct*, elevation, plan, and cross sections, plate from G. Eiffel, *Mémoire sur le viaduc de Garabit*, Paris, 1889.

68 *Garabit Viaduct*, elevation of the masonry piers, pen and watercolor, Paris, Archives nationales.

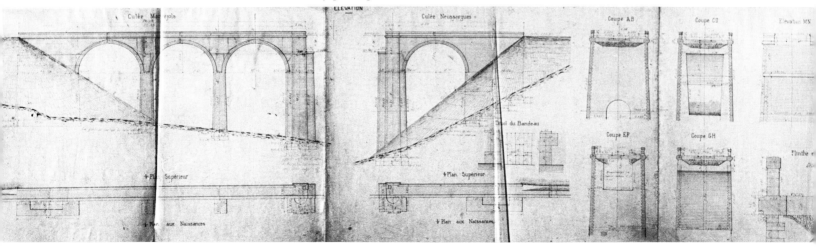

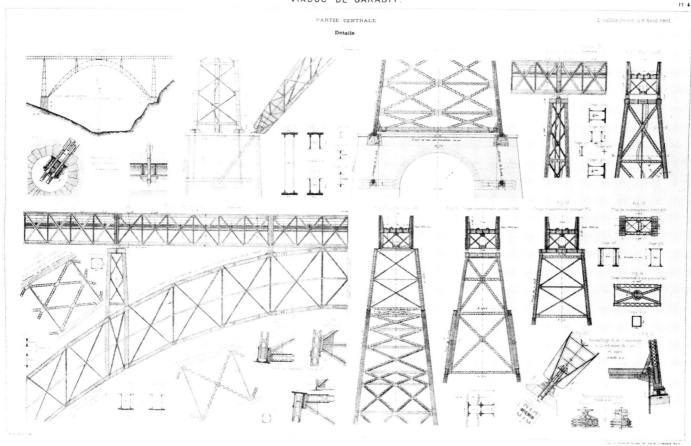

69 *Garabit Viaduct*, details of the central section, plate from G. Eiffel, *Mémoire sur le viaduc de Garabit*, Paris, 1889.

70 *Garabit Viaduct*, assembly of the arch, securing of the arch and the deck during assembly, plate from G. Eiffel, *Mémoire sur le viaduc de Garabit*, Paris, 1889.

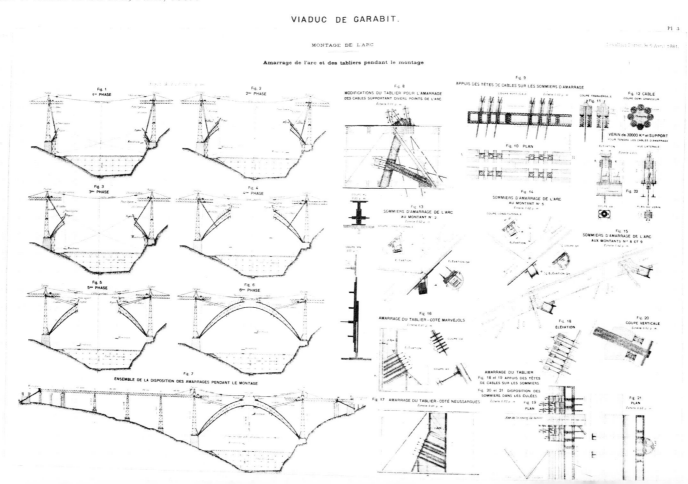

Garonne, and, after being made a head of section in Eiffel's company, on all the major structures entrusted to the company up to the tower.

The origin and construction of the Garabit viaduct are well documented thanks to the numerous files which are now in the French National Archives, and in particular to the twenty-three boxes containing the detailed plans; apart from those for the 300-meter tower, these are the only complete set of plans for a work carried out by Gustave Eiffel.[69] In his *Mémoire* of 1880, Eiffel describes the whole of the structure as consisting of "a large metal viaduct, extended at its two ends by masonry viaducts acting as the abutments." The track was 122.20 meters above the deepest part of the valley; the metal part itself consisted of a straight-girder deck, supported as follows:

1) on the masonry projections of the viaducts at either end;
2) on metal piers, for the parts above the sides of the valley;
3) above the Thalweg, on five supports set up on the extrados of a great arch with a span of 165 meters, by means of two bents and intermediate supports.[70]

The highest pier was 89.64 meters high and was formed "from a masonry base 25 meters wide and 28.90 meters high, on top of which stands the metal part 61 meters high."

Construction was carried out according to the technique tested on the Douro bridge, "that is, by suspending each of the half-arches on steel cables fixed to the deck, and fastening all the components to one another in space by assembling them as a series of cantilevers. The back ends of the deck were themselves fixed to the abutment blocks by other cables, which could be adjusted to enable the front parts, which were attached to the parts of the arch under construction, to be moved."[71]

72 *Garabit Viaduct*, great pier, photograph from G. Eiffel, *Mémoire sur le viaduc de Garabit*, Paris, 1889.

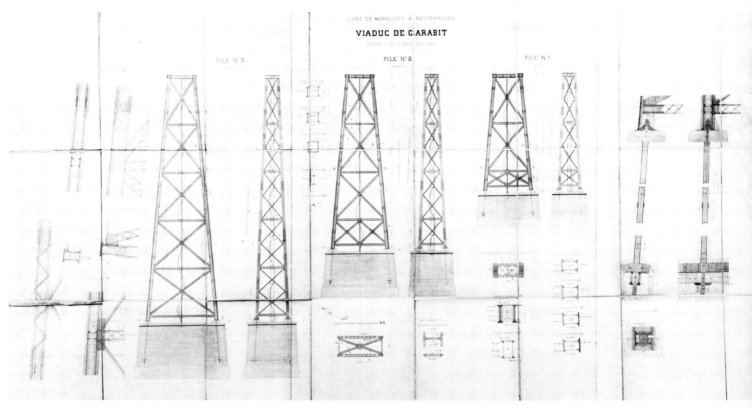

73 *Garabit Viaduct*, general view and details of the piers, plate from G. Eiffel, *Mémoire sur le viaduc de Garabit*, Paris, 1889.

74 *Garabit Viaduct*, general view and details of the central section, print, Paris, Archives nationales.

75 *Garabit Viaduct*, details of the downward curve of the ▷ arch, photograph from G. Eiffel, *Mémoire sur le viaduc de Garabit*, Paris, 1889.

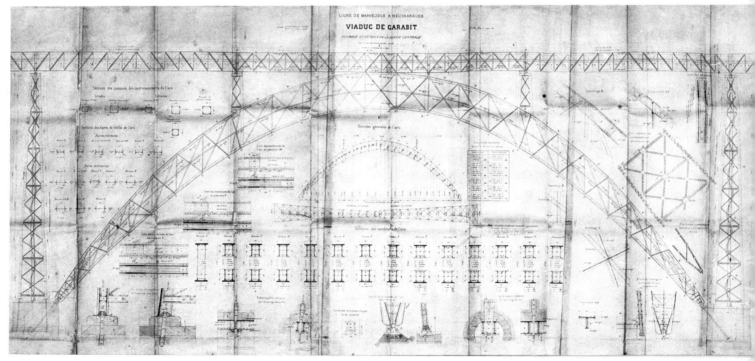

76, 77 *Garabit Viaduct*, assembly of the central section of the arch, photographs, Paris, Musée d'Orsay, Eiffel collection.

78, 79 *Garabit Viaduct*, general views with details of the arch and the hoisting jigs, photographs, Paris, Musée d'Orsay, Eiffel collection.

Although it uses the same model and method of construction as the Douro bridge, the Garabit viaduct was not simply a repetition of this bridge in a different place, for Eiffel was to introduce various improvements. Thus, in this type of structure, the railroad track had previously always been placed on the upper part of the deck, so that if the train was derailed it would only meet a light parapet which could not prevent it from falling; Eiffel now placed it 1.66 meters below the upper flange plate of the girders, so that these girders formed a solid wall on both sides capable of keeping in vehicles if they came off the rails.[72]

Major Works

When the ninety-year-old Eiffel looked back on the whole of his work, placing more emphasis on his discoveries in the fields of meteorology and aerodynamics than on his career as an engineer, he

80 *Garabit Viaduct*, general view, photograph, Paris, Musée d'Orsay, Eiffel collection.

81 *Handbill "G. Eiffel, engineer and builder,"* with Garabit ▷ Viaduct.

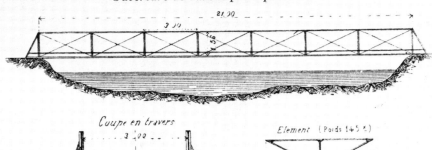

87

82 *Bordeaux Bridge*, perspective view, photograph tinted in oils, Paris, Musée d'Orsay, Eiffel collection.

83 *Cubzac Bridge*, elevation, pen and watercolor, Paris, Archives nationales.

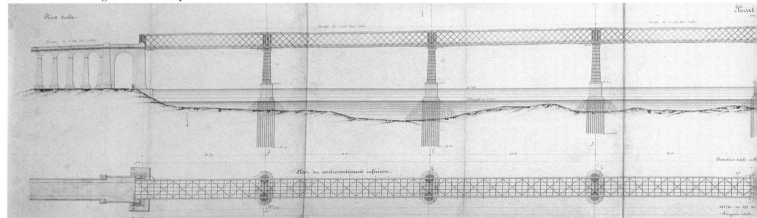

84 Albert Schickedanz, *Szeged Bridge*, perspective view, watercolor, Paris, Musée d'Orsay, Eiffel collection.

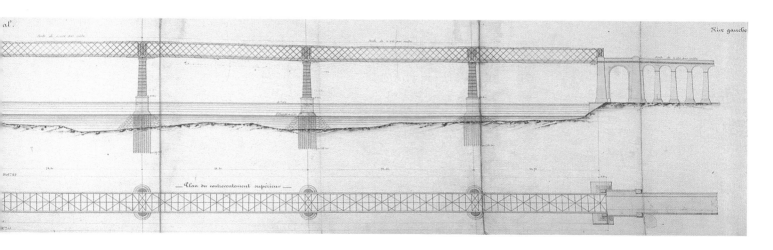

mentioned the Cubzac bridge over the Dordogne only for the sake of the method of assembly used. The new bridge, which had been decided on in 1879 and designed by the Highways Department engineer Charles de Sansac, was in fact to retain "the outline of the old suspension bridge," was to be supported on "openwork cast-iron piers with a quite characteristic appearance," and was to be joined to "the masonry approach viaducts which brought the roadway to ground level." This was an awkward and delicate, though lucrative task; in fact the deck of the new bridge had to follow the old slope, and the rolling out therefore had to be done horizontally "on wooden props of very

different heights, resulting in a lack of stability which was always dangerous." The length of the bridge (552 meters in eight spans), its weight (3,000 tonnes), and the instability of the old piers forced Eiffel to innovate. The first three spans were built out from each of the two banks. "For the two central spans, the gradient was different and a new method of assembly had to be employed—by cantilever, which Monsieur Eiffel was the first to use in France, and which can be summed up thus: On one part of the bridge girder, which has already been constructed in its final position, the iron components following it are bolted onto it as cantilevers; once they have been riveted, they are used as

85, 86 *Cubzac Bridge*, central elevation, elevation of a pier, longitudinal and transverse sections, pen and watercolor, Paris, Archives nationales.

87 *La Tardes Viaduct*, diagram of the different stages of launching, pen and watercolor, Paris, Archives nationales.

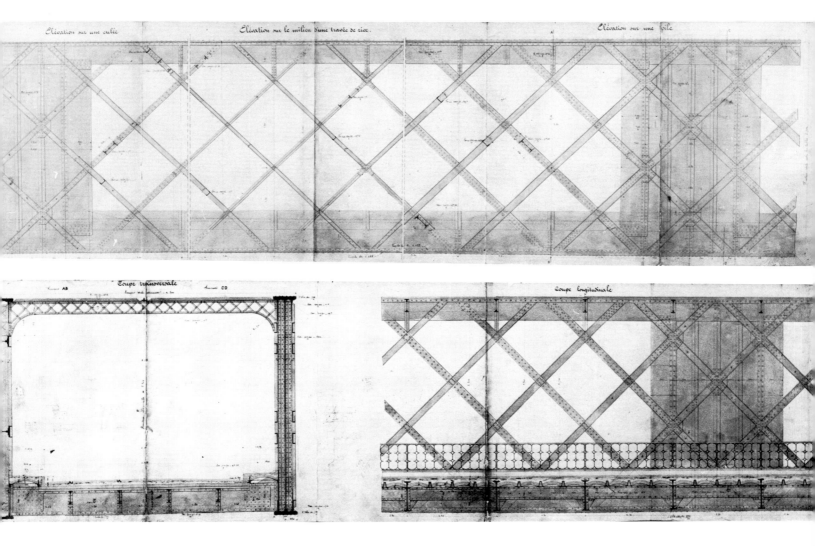

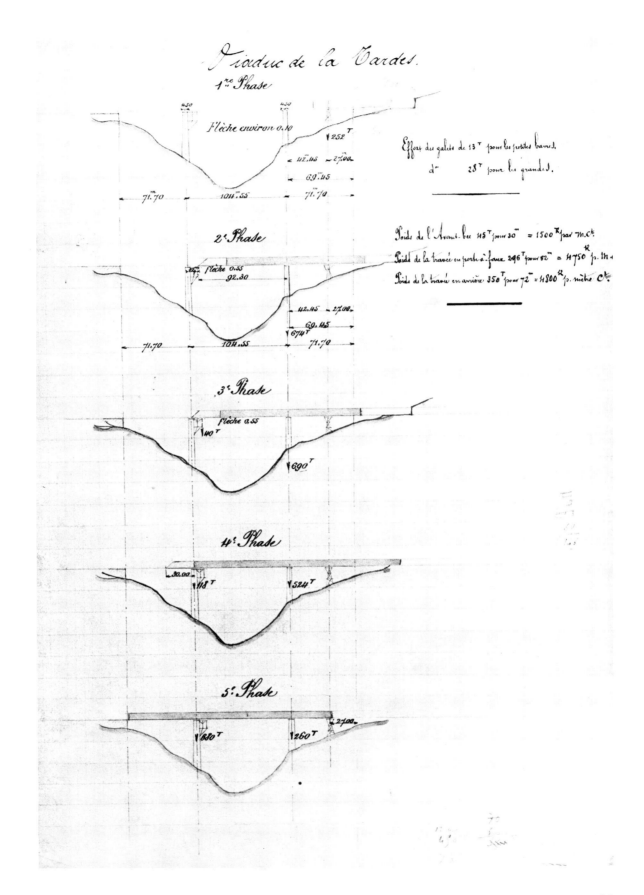

Viaduc de la Tardes.

1re Phase

Flèche environ 0.10

2e Phase

flèche 0.55
92.30

3e Phase

flèche 0.55

4e Phase

30.00

5e Phase

Effort des galets de 13 T pour les petites travées.
d° 28 T pour les grandes.

Poids de l'Avant-bec 45 T pour 30 m = 1500 K par m.ct
Poids de la travée en porte-à-faux 296 T pour 82 m = 4750 K p. m.
Poids de la travée en arrière 350 T pour 72 m = 4800 K p. mètre ct

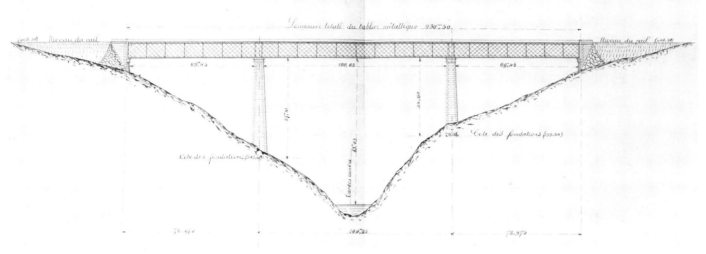

Viaduc de la Tardes
Ensemble.

88   *La Tardes Viaduct*, elevation, pen and ink, Paris, Archives nationales.

89   *La Tardes Viaduct*, photograph, Paris, Musée d'Orsay, Eiffel collection.

90   *Seine Barrage at Port-Mort under construction.* ▷

91   *Seine Barrage at Port-Mort.* ▷

92–95 *Bridge over the Saône at Collonges* (Paris, Lyons, and Mediterranean Railroad Company), 1887, photographs, Paris, Musée d'Orsay, Eiffel collection.

the new supports for bolting on the following sections. Moving gradually out in this way, the successive sections of the span are assembled entirely in the air, until it reaches the nearest support, when by means of hydraulic jacks the bridge is raised by the amount it had dropped through bending. For the Cubzac bridge, the sections were moved forward in this way over a length of 72.80 meters as far as the arch of the central pier, where the girders of the two spans cantilevered out were joined together (fig. 14)." With some pride, Eiffel justified going into such great detail on these processes "because they all involve significant improvements on the processes in use up until then, and because they are the work of Monsieur Eiffel."[73] Such modesty is touching.

But Eiffel's mastery as a builder was put to a stiff test during the work on the Tardes viaduct, on the line from Montluçon to Eyguerande, commissioned by the Orléans Company; he would go back to the rolling-out system he had introduced in 1869 on the Sioule viaduct. The depth of the valley—the track was 80 meters above the bottom of the river— the length of the metal deck (250 meters), and above all the lay of the land, which obliged the train to enter and come off the viaduct on a curve and therefore required the construction of a trough in the straight stretch of the track, rendered the task particularly arduous. A drawing preserved in the French National Archives shows the "ideal" progression of the five stages of rolling out,[74] but during the night of January 26–27, 1884, when the front of the deck was still in the form of a 53-meter cantilever from the masonry pier of the right bank, a storm blew up, and overturned the metal deck. In all his career Eiffel had never experienced such an

96 *Liberty lighting the world*, detail of the base of one of the principal supports; fixing for the tie rods; construction diagram for the statue, plate from the *Génie Civil*, 1883.

97 *Statue of Liberty under construction*, engraving published ▷ in the *Génie Civil*, 1883.

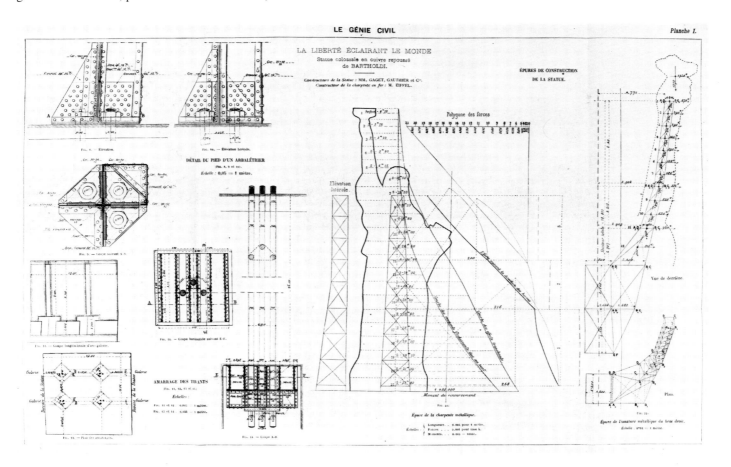

98 *Publicity leaflet from the Maison Gaget, Monduit, and Co. with the Statue of Liberty and Millet's Vercingétorix.*

99 *Nice Observatory, Great Equatorial* ▷ *Telescope,* elevation and cross section, pen and watercolor, Paris, Archives nationales.

accident. He was freed of all responsibility, the State undertook to pay for the damage, and construction was completed without further incident the following year; nevertheless, there is no mention of the accident in Eiffel's *Biographie.*

On the other hand, Eiffel remained extremely proud of the Szeged road bridge in Hungary, which he constructed after winning an international competition opened at the end of 1880 "between the major construction companies in France and abroad." Aided by the engineer Janos Feketehazy, he gave his structure "a span of 110 meters, depressed to the thirteenth, which has a striking lightness"[75] and which strangely foreshadowed the Alexander III bridge built for the Universal Exhibition of 1900.

The failure to win another project—a road bridge at Oporto, for which his former partner Théophile Seyrig won the contract—did not affect the company's good business in the slightest; orders were flooding in, for metal bridges in France (including the Morannes bridge in 1885, the first French steel bridge) and in Cochin-China, where there were many more of the increasingly successful "economical portable bridges," the stock exchange at the Crédit Lyonnais bank (1881), a

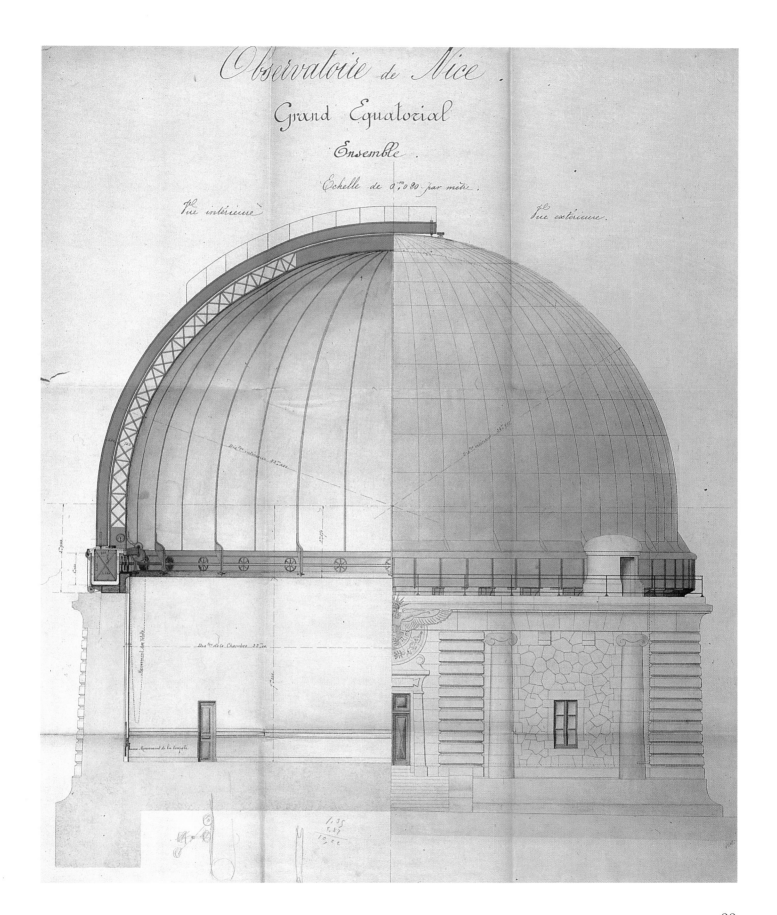

Observatoire de Nice.

Grand Equatorial

Ensemble.

Echelle de 0.^m020 par mètre.

Vue intérieure — *Vue extérieure.*

great metal hall with three levels of offices opening onto it, and for the dam on the Seine at Port-Mort (1884), "with its curtains maintained by reinforcements 13 meters high, supported themselves by a strong deck 204 meters long and 12.20 meters wide."[76]

Although the Statue of Liberty seems to many to stand apart from the rest of Eiffel's work, he himself saw it differently. Despite the "artistic" covering which completely concealed the work he had carried out, it can nevertheless be seen as a continuation of his earlier work, as he explained himself: "By analogy with metal piers, which are especially calculated to resist wind stresses, I may cite the example of the huge Statue of Liberty erected by Monsieur Bartholdi in New York harbor."[77]

The monumental statue was designed by Auguste Bartholdi, an active "entrepreneur," but a very ordinary and mediocre sculptor, and Edouard de Laboulaye, a lecturer at the Collège de France and a fervent republican, to celebrate at once French participation in America's independence, the close links between the two countries, and the republican ideal of liberty. It was conceived as early as 1865, and begun in 1877; part of it was shown at the Universal Exhibition in 1878. It was completed in Paris in 1884, transported in separate pieces, and finally unveiled on Bedloe's Island in 1886.

It had been decided that the statue, which was to be constructed in the Monduit workshops (which had produced the roofing for Garnier's Opera House, the Paris City Hall, and the Palais de Justice in Brussels), would be made of embossed copper supported by an iron framework; as Charles Talansier noted in Le Génie Civil,[78] "embossing makes possible large pieces with the lowest possible weight in relation to their volume." In 1881, Bartholdi applied directly to Eiffel, maintaining that his studies of the wind resistance of metal constructions made him "the obvious person to construct the iron carcass,"[79] pretending to be unaware that Viollet-le-Duc, who had died in 1879, and who had designed the framework for Millet's gigantic Vercingétorix, had undertaken the first calculations in this field. Eiffel agreed to work for the sculptor, under "the conditions of strict economy which circumstances imposed," designing "an iron framework which would serve as a support for the whole of the copper envelope" and would form "a sort of large pylon secured at four points to the masonry base supporting the statue."[80] The high elasticity of the envelope provided for the inevitable expansion. Furthermore, "so that each metal can expand freely, the iron reinforcements, instead of being riveted onto the statue, are simply held in copper sheaths which are themselves riveted to the exterior." To offset the electrical activity resulting from the sea wind and rainstorms, when the statue was finally assembled the builders placed "small copper plates covered with rags suitably coated with red lead between the sheets of copper and the iron framework"—a process frequently used for the sheathing of ships.[81]

As we have seen, Eiffel's opinion of his own works varied. Leaving the tower aside, there were those he was particularly fond of, such as the Douro and Garabit viaducts, and also the Pest station and the Szeged bridge; he comes back to these constantly in his notes, his lectures, and his correspondence. The Statue of Liberty does not number among them; he mentions it mainly so as to ensure that it is not attributed entirely to Bartholdi, but he kept no account or memento of it. In the substantial collection left to the Musée d'Orsay by his descendants, there is nothing, or almost nothing, on this monument, except for an offprint of Charles Talansier's article in Le Génie Civil. By contrast, the dome of the great equatorially mounted telescope in Nice, which he worked on in 1885–86, an admirable achievement, was one of his "favorites," "one of Monsieur Eiffel's most interesting works,"[82] as he did not hesitate to write in his Biographie.

The construction of the Nice Observatory[83] resulted from the meeting of Raphael Bischoffsheim and Loewy, from the Bureau des Longitudes, shortly before the fall of the Empire. Bischoffsheim, who came from a family of bankers and was colossally rich, had been trained as a civil engineer and, being interested in science, became its Maecenas. To begin with, he had a small angled equatorial built at his expense at the Paris Observatory. In 1879, still following Loewy's advice, he engaged on a more ambitious project: that of endowing France with an observatory equipped with the most sophisticated scientific instruments, on a suitable site. He took upon himself the purchase of the land at Mont-Gros, on the hills above Nice, and the costs of constructing all the buildings; since he also wished to make them a work of art, he called on Charles Garnier, who had built a large villa for him at Bordighera in 1878. The ensemble was very extensive, comprising administrative buildings as well as observation pavilions. Work began in 1881; Eiffel's contribution was limited to the most important building, and the one which Garnier had made the most monumental, the pavilion for the great equatorial (this pavilion alone cost one million francs). Garnier had been charmed by a previous rejected project of Eiffel's for the reconstruction of the dome of the Paris Observatory, and it was he himself who called Eiffel in.

On the Palladian "base" designed by Garnier, Eiffel erected a dome with a diameter of 22.40 meters, "which makes it the largest in existence." "Its success is due to the particular feature that instead of revolving on rollers, it is supported by a ring-shaped float devised by Monsieur Eiffel. This float is immersed, like a ship, in a reservoir which is also ring-shaped, so that a child could shift this great mass of 100,000 kilograms with one hand. A system of backup rollers adjacent to the float, in case the latter is being repaired, allows the dome to be moved by the conventional method. It goes without saying that the liquid used will not freeze."[84]

The construction of the large telescope was to be the only occasion when Gustave Eiffel and Charles Garnier worked together, or at least on the same project. This was a symbolic meeting between the two men, one personifying the engineer, and the other the architect, then as they do for us today. We shall describe later how Charles Garnier's acid remarks in 1857 on the use of iron in architecture, on the one hand, and the construction of the Eiffel tower in 1889 and its preservation in the heart of Paris, on the other, were to open and close one of the liveliest debates of the century: Art or Industry, Stone versus iron; or even, and for us more particularly, Charles Garnier versus Gustave Eiffel.

The 300-Meter Tower

"This tower is Monsieur Eiffel's magnum opus, and is a symbol of strength and difficulties overcome." It was thus that Gustave Eiffel was to introduce the lengthy chapter devoted to this monument in his *Biographie*.[1] He considered that it would be pointless to describe it, in view of the vast number of reproductions available the world over, but he laid emphasis on the experiments which it had made possible in aerodynamics and, from 1905 on, in wireless telegraphy. The tower was not a useless object, a mere attraction for the Universal Exhibition; it rendered invaluable services to science. This is why Eiffel only speaks "in general terms of its history, its importance, and its utility."[2]

"The idea of a tower of great height was not a new one," Alfred Picard noted forthrightly in his *Rapport Général*[3] on the 1889 Exhibition. Eugène-Melchior de Vogüé, who made pertinent remarks about all the displays of 1889, observed more discerningly that "the idea had been taking shape gradually in the minds of engineers for some years, waiting to come out into the light."[4] In fact, it seems that for everybody except for Eiffel, who ignored previous attempts, it was the realization of an old dream. The tower was not due simply to Gustave Eiffel; it came at its appointed time, prompted by technological advances and political contingencies, and, more vaguely, by the spirit of the times. In those times of fervent or disputed republicanism, when people wanted to celebrate the centenary of the French Revolution in splendid fashion, the tower seemed to some like the victory of the masonic lodges over the clerics, "a proper

100 *Gustave Eiffel c. 1889*, watercolor (sketch for *Vanity Fair?*), Paris, Musée d'Orsay, Eiffel collection.

7ᵉ volume.   Nᵒ 351. — 10 c.   Un an : 6 fr.

LES HOMMES D'AUJOURD'HUI

DESSIN DE LUQUE
TEXTE DE PIERRE ET PAUL

Bureaux : Librairie Vanier, 19, quai Saint-Michel, Paris

GUSTAVE EIFFEL

101 Luque, *Gustave Eiffel*, cover of *Men of Today*, 1889, Paris, Musée d'Orsay, Eiffel collection.

102 *Caricature of Gustave Eiffel*, published in the *Central* (1889). "By the magnitude of the work the greatness of the man is measured." Paris, Musée d'Orsay, Eiffel collection.

GUSTAVE EIFFEL (1855)

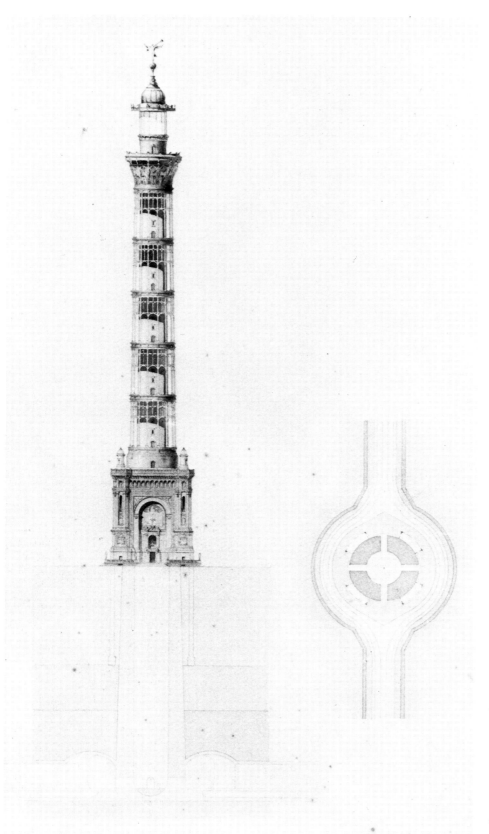

103 Jules Bourdais, *Design for a monumental lighthouse for Paris,* plan and elevation, watercolor, Paris, Musée d'Orsay.

mystification for the priests, the revenge for the failure of the masons of Senaar so long ago."[5] All-powerful science was building the Tower of Babel which the God of the Bible had put a stop to.

But without going back to the "Tower of Babel, of great renown" (Alfred Picard's ironic phrase), some often-quoted antecedents should be mentioned. These start with the proposal made in 1833 by the British engineer Trevithick to erect a huge cast-iron openwork column 1,000 feet (304.80 meters) high "to commemorate the Reform Bill passed by Parliament the year before." Trevithick died in the year that the plans were presented, and the project came to nothing. Eiffel's structure owes more to this circular column than to the Washington obelisk or than to Bourdais's Tour Soleil, which we shall discuss later; the generalized use of metal and the interplay between solids and voids are common to both structures. Picard, who is more forthcoming than Eiffel on the origins of the 300-meter tower, describes Trevithick's column thus: "It was to rest on a stone base 18 meters high, and would have a diameter of 30 meters at the base and 3.60 meters at the top. It was to be topped by a capital with a platform 15 meters in diameter, bearing a statue 12 meters high. Fifteen hundred sheets of cast iron 3 meters square and 0.05 meters thick, with an inner diameter of 1.80 meters would have been used to make it; they would have been assembled using straps and bolts. The total weight of the metal section would have been about 6,000 tonnes. An elevator, placed inside the column and driven by compressed air, would travel the 300 meters in five minutes, at a speed of one meter per second."[6]

The Washington obelisk, started in 1848, was finished only in 1885, after many setbacks (when the height of 46 meters had been reached, it was realized that the monument was leaning perceptibly); it comes a poor second to Trevithick's project. It is 169 meters high, and made of white marble, and in fact only very distantly related to the future Eiffel Tower. Another project for a tower 304 meters high, designed for the Universal Exhibition in Philadelphia by the engineers Clarke and Reeves, which came to nothing; a proposal to

104 Jules Bourdais, *Design for a monumental lighthouse for Paris*, elevation, watercolor, Paris, Musée d'Orsay.

build a 200-meter wooden tower in Brussels; the construction of the Mole Antonelliana, 170 meters high, in Turin; a proposal for an enormous lighthouse for Paris—such were the stages which led gradually to the construction of Eiffel's tower.

Forerunners

In 1885, Jules Bourdais, taking up an idea put forward by the engineer Sébillot in 1881, for a 300-meter tower "topped by an electric furnace which would light up Paris," submitted a design to the Exhibition Commission; it was to be a granite column resting on a base 66 meters high and 30 meters square, and was to be topped by an electric beacon 50 meters high, made entirely of metal. "The tower itself consists of a central masonry core, covered with sheet metal or embossed copper; its average diameter is 28 meters, and its cross section decreases from the base to the top. It is divided into five tiers, each one decorated with columns. A huge capital crowns the structure."[7] Objections were not slow to be raised: stability, resistance to crushing, the proposed structure's weight. Tactlessly, Bourdais ignored them: "As regards stability, and, more particularly, with respect to wind resistance, Monsieur Bourdais used a formula which he says he has tested in practice more than once, and whose results, according to him, agree with the dimensions used in the tallest buildings in the world. We shall accept his results without questioning them." One could hardly be more offhand. As for resistance to crushing, "the dimensions of the tower give no ground for fear, since the height of the tower does not exceed the maximum height permitted by theory [...]. Thus there is no cause for anxiety here."[8] But, in addition to these brilliant demonstrations which allowed for no reply, Bourdais produced a weighty argument: Eiffel's rival project, a vulgar iron structure, would cost 21,700,000 francs; while his granite tower was true architecture for a mere 3,120,000 francs. There was no question of foundations—the 320-square-meter base was apparently to rest

105 Jules Bourdais, *Design for a monumental lighthouse for Paris*, maquette, Paris, Musée d'Orsay.

directly on the ground—and not a word about the elevators or the electrical equipment necessary for the operation of the beacon.

Leaving aside the whimsical aspect of the architect's estimates, which would take all credibility away from his proposal, we must nevertheless dwell on Sébillot's extraordinary idea of endowing Paris with a huge lighthouse which would easily have illuminated the Bois de Boulogne, and all of Neuilly and Levallois right up to the Seine: "an electric furnace with a power of 2,000,000 Caral burners would be installed in the upper part of the tower [...] consisting of 100 lamps arranged in a ring, equipped with specially shaped reflectors, all calculated to send out the same amount of light to each of the twenty-four equal-sized zones into which the designer has divided the capital."[9] A witty journalist noted that "given the height of our houses, the narrowness of our streets, and the fact that they rarely lie in line with the rays coming from the foot of the column," only the roofs would be brightly lit; "so that, by a reversal which the designers certainly did not intend, it will be the cats who will see clearly and the passersby who will not see at all."[10]

Bourdais and Sébillot's tower would make it possible to see as clearly at midnight as in broad daylight; this was not its only advantage. At 300 meters above the ground, the air is so pure that a veritable hospital could have been installed in the upper levels, so that patients who wanted to take an "aero-therapy" treatment would not have to travel far.

The Genesis of Eiffel's Project

Faced with so many utilitarian, scientific, and medical virtues, Gustave Eiffel's proposal seemed both more symbolic and more trivial. "As Monsieur Eiffel envisaged it, this colossal structure was to be a dazzling demonstration of France's industrial power, to be evidence of our enormous progress in the art of metal construction, to celebrate the astonishingly rapid development of civil engineering over this century, to attract many visitors and make a substantial contribution to the success of the great peaceful meetings organized to commemorate the centenary of 1789."[11] There are two versions of the origin of the project: the "official" one recorded in the *Rapport*, the other given

by Eiffel himself; as in the case of the Douro bridge or the Statue of Liberty, he found it difficult to accept that he had not been the only begetter.

Alfred Picard's *Rapport* describes Gustave Eiffel taking up the tempting project devised by two of his company's engineers: "Monsieur Nouguier and Monsieur Koechlin, engineers with the Eiffel company, and Monsieur Sauvestre, architect, had drawn up a preliminary plan for a great metal tower 300 meters high. This venture was just the thing to tempt a skillful, experienced, and daring builder like Monsieur Eiffel. He had no hesitation in taking responsibility for it and presenting firm proposals to the Minister for Trade and Industry with a view to including the tower in the Universal Exhibition of 1889."[12]

In his *Biographie*, Eiffel put himself at the top of the list, deliberately refusing to make any distinction between designer and contractor: "In 1886, Monsieur Eiffel, together with Monsieur Nouguier and Monsieur Koechlin, engineers with his company, and Monsieur Sauvestre, architect, submitted a pilot project for a 300-meter-high tower to Monsieur Lockroy, Minister for Trade and General Commissioner for the Exhibition of 1889; they accepted responsibility for its construction, within clearly defined price- and time-limits."[13] It was in fact as early as 1884 that Nouguier and Koechlin, discussing possible attractions for the 1889 Exhibition between themselves, had come up with the idea of "a very high tower";[14] on June 6 of the same year, Koechlin drew a sketch of the construction they had thought up, "a great pylon consisting of four lattice girders standing apart at the base and coming together at the top, joined to one another by metal trusses at regular intervals."[15] To show the scale of his monument, he conscientiously piled up beside it Notre-Dame, the Statue of Liberty, the Arc de Triomphe, three columns the height of the column in the Place Vendôme, and finally a six-story apartment block. Not long afterwards the two engineers asked the architect Stephen Sauvestre to give architectural form to their quick sketch, in short, to make the pylon a tower. Sauvestre, who with Eiffel had created the pavilion for the Paris Gas Company at the 1878 Exhibition, and was director of the Eiffel company's architectural office, inserted an arch between the base and the first platform, where he put in a large glass-paneled hall, crowned the whole with a light onion-shaped roof, and scattered the customary sculptures here

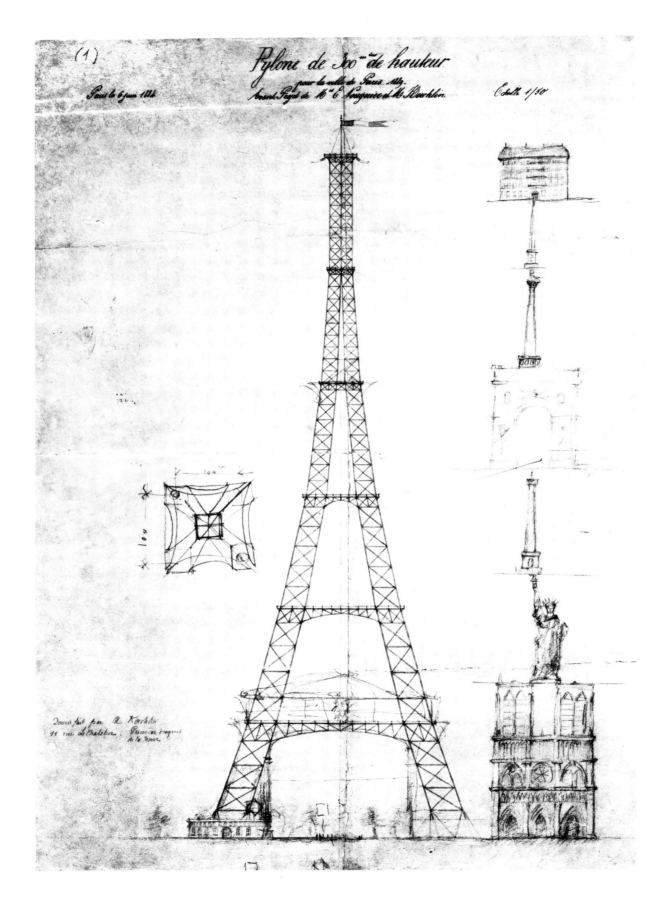

106 Maurice Koechlin, *"Pylon 300 meters high for the city of Paris. 1889, preliminary draft by Messrs. E. Nouguier and M. Koechlin,"* June 6, 1884, pencil, private collection, loaned to the Zurich Polytechnikum.

107 *"Gallia, Metal Tower 300 meters high,"* pencil, Paris, Musée d'Orsay, Eiffel collection.

and there. Eiffel, won over to the project, then bought "the exclusive right to the patent" from his colleagues and, without any further ado, launched himself into the "usual formalities."[16]

On March 30, 1885, Eiffel read a paper to the Société des Ingénieurs Civils entitled *Tour en fer de 300 mètres de hauteur destinée à l'Exposition de 1889*, which, when printed, specified that it was "A project presented by Monsieur G. Eiffel, engineer and contractor, drawn up by Monsieur E. Nouguier and Monsieur M. Koechlin, engineers with Eiffel's company, and by Monsieur Sauvestre, architect." As he noted in the introduction, "there are now few people who are not familiar with the main idea of this project"; it had been presented at the Exhibition of Decorative Arts in the fall of 1884, was already being debated and criticized, and already had its opponents as well as its supporters. It was now time to bring in the necessary technical specifications: "By now the question has been properly put; the different objections which could arise have been put forward, as has the evidence about the applications which are realistically possible." The starting point for this proposal was the study of the metal piers supporting railroad viaducts; these piers had already been lengthened more than might have been expected in the construction of the framework for the Statue of Liberty, and Eiffel's study had led him to believe that "their height could be extended considerably beyond what has been achieved so far."[17]

The main difficulty was still to overcome wind resistance. Since the lattice bars normally used for this purpose in viaducts would be "practically useless" here, "it would [...] be most profitable to do away completely with these additional components, which would be relatively very heavy, and to give the pier such a form that all the shearing forces were concentrated in its ribs. This would be done by reducing the structure to four great legs with no wind bracing, joined only by a few deep horizontal trusses very widely spaced." In order to do away with the lattice bars, therefore, it would be enough to "make the legs curve in such a way that the tangents to them, drawn from points at the same height, will always meet at the point through which passes the resultant of the wind stresses on that part of the pier which is above the points in question." There followed a description of the tower as sketched by Nouguier and Koechlin, and then Sauvestre, with its carcass "of four rising

members forming the edges of a pyramid with curved surfaces," a 4,200-square-meter glass-paneled gallery on the first level, a 900-square-meter gallery on the second, and finally "a 250-square-meter glass-paneled dome with an outside balcony," a point with a magnificent view, but also the place for scientific experiments. The omnipresent metal would be set off by "embellishments of varying color" attached to the spandrels of the arches 80 meters wide and 50 meters high which are "the principal element of the decoration."[18] The cost of the whole was estimated at 3,155,000 francs (it was to cost two and a half times as much, but in the printed copy of his lecture in the Musée d'Orsay's Eiffel collection, Eiffel had already corrected the initial 3 to a 5); it would weigh 4,810 tonnes (he corrected this in pencil to 6,500; the tower in fact weighs 7,300 tonnes); he added that "experience from my work allows me to state that the construction will not take more than one year"[19] (it took twenty-six months).

Although certain that metal was to be used—apart from the advantages mentioned above, it also made the tower easier to move after the exhibition ended—Eiffel was still hesitating between iron and steel. At that time, he inclined towards iron, which was heavier and more resistant to buckling, and was easier to work than steel, but he nevertheless reserved his final decision. The one thing he was certain of was that the use of masonry alone, as proposed by Bourdais (for he had to take care to eliminate his rival), would render the project impossible. The ancient civilizations, the Middle Ages, and the Renaissance had pushed the use of stone to the limits of boldness, "and it hardly seems possible to go much further than our precursors using the same materials."[20] A few years later Huysmans, writing very critically of contemporary constructions, including both Garnier's Opera and Davioud and Bourdais's Trocadero, also condemned stone which seemed to him "exhausted, drained by repeated use."[21] For this end of the century, an era of "utilitarian ribaldry," there was only one material which could be embodied in monuments to symbolize "its vitality and its sadness, its shrewdess and its love of money, in structures

108 *"Design for a commemorative monument to be built at the 1889 Universal Exhibition,"* plate from the *Génie Civil,* December 13, 1884.

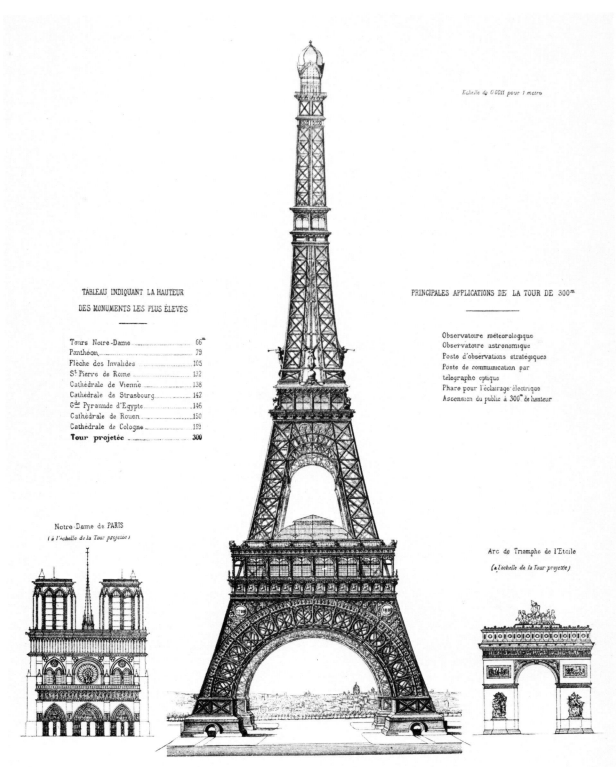

Echelle de 0.0011 pour 1 metre

TABLEAU INDIQUANT LA HAUTEUR

DES MONUMENTS LES PLUS ÉLEVÉS

Tours Notre-Dame	66ᵐ
Panthéon	79
Flèche des Invalides	105
St Pierre de Rome	132
Cathédrale de Vienne	138
Cathédrale de Strasbourg	142
Gde Pyramide d'Egypte	146
Cathédrale de Rouen	150
Cathédrale de Cologne	159
Tour projetée	**300**

PRINCIPALES APPLICATIONS DE LA TOUR DE 300ᵐ

Observatoire météorologique
Observatoire astronomique
Poste d'observations stratégiques
Poste de communication par
telegraphe optique
Phare pour l'éclairage électrique
Ascension du public à 300ᵐ de hauteur

Notre-Dame de PARIS
(à l'échelle de la Tour projetée)

Arc de Triomphe de l'Etoile
(à l'échelle de la Tour projetée)

PROJET DE MONUMENT COMMÉMORATIF
A ÉRIGER A L'EXPOSITION UNIVERSELLE DE 1889
Presente par M G EIFFEL Ingenieur-Constructeur

Projet de Messieurs E NOUGUIER, M KOECHLIN, ingrs de la Maison EIFFEL et S SAUVESTRE, Architecte

which would be sullen and hard, but in any case new";[22] and this material was iron. Only metal could give the planned tower the appropriate appearance: "the legs, before joining together at that lofty summit, seem to spring out of the ground, and somehow to be molded by the action of the wind itself."[23]

The final weighty argument for building this monument was its usefulness, which Eiffel stressed constantly; to support his proposal he would quote the favorable opinions of well-known scientists— that of Hervé-Mangon emphasizing the significance of such a venture for meteorology, that of Admiral Mouchez, the Director of the Observatory, who stressed its value for the "study of the lower layers of the atmosphere," or that of Colonel Perrier, who confirmed that such a tower would render considerable services to optical telegraphy. To sum up, Eiffel recalled the indisputable possibility of carrying out the construction, the relatively modest price, the scientific value, and the certain popular success of the tower, and concluded by saying that his structure would symbolize "not only the art of the modern Engineer, but also the century of Industry and Science in which we are living, and for which the way was prepared by the great scientific movement of the end of the eighteenth century and by the Revolution of 1789, to which this monument will be built as an expression of France's gratitude."[24]

Until the spring of 1886, there was little progress. Then with the reelection of Jules Grévy as President of the Republic at the end of 1885, the successive appointments of Freycinet as President of the Upper Chamber, of Sadi Carnot as Treasury Minister, and above all of Edouard Lockroy as Minister for Trade, the situation was finally unblocked. The Chamber of Deputies passed the budget for the Universal Exhibition and on May 1, 1886, Lockroy stopped the open competition program and inserted the following clause which to all intents and purposes guaranteed victory to Eiffel: "The candidates must investigate the possibility of erecting a square-based iron tower, 125 meters square at the base and 300 meters high, on the Champ de Mars. They must draw out this tower on the plan of the Champ de Mars, and if they deem it fitting, they may submit another plan without the said tower."[25]

On May 12, a committee was set up to examine Eiffel's project; it was chaired by Lockroy himself,

and included Alphand, Director of Works of the City of Paris; G. Berger, a former commissioner for the International Exhibitions; the architect Emmanuel Brune, lecturer at the Ecole des Beaux-Arts; the engineers V. Contamin, lecturer at the Ecole Centrale, Hersent, President of the Société des Ingénieurs Civils, and Molinos; the scientists Hervé-Mangon, Admiral Mouchez, and Phillips; and politicians like the deputy Ménard-Dorian. At least two members, Hervé-Mangon and Admiral Mouchez, had publicly declared themselves in favor of Eiffel's project as much as a year before.

On May 15, a subcommittee consisting only of Phillips, a member of the Academy of Sciences and a retired Inspector General of Mines; Collignon, a lecturer at the Ecole Polytechnique; and Contamin was nominated to compose a report on the different projects which had been submitted: that of Eiffel, of course, that of Bourdais, and also those of Boucher, Henry, Marion, Pochet, Robert, Rouyer, and Speyser.

By the second session, on June 12, the report drawn up by the subcommittee was presented by Collignon, and the rival projects were put aside as unworkable or insufficiently well studied. At Alphand's proposal, it was unanimously declared that "the tower to be built for the 1889 Universal Exhibition should clearly have a distinctive character, and should be an original masterpiece of work in metal, and that only the Eiffel Tower seemed to satisfy these requirements fully. Consequently the committee, within the limits of the purely technical mandate conferred upon it, has proposed to the minister that the proposed Eiffel Tower should be adopted, with the double reservation that the engineering contractor should study the elevator mechanism in more detail, and that three specialists, Messieurs Mascart, Becquerel, and Berger, be requested to give their opinions on the measures to be taken with regard to the electrical phenomena which could arise."[26]

All that remained was to choose to exact site. For some time there had been hesitation between the Champ de Mars and the Trocadero; in the overall plan presented for the installation of the Universal

109 "Design competition for the 1889 Exhibition," designs by Raulin, Deperthes, Cassien-Bernard and Nachon.

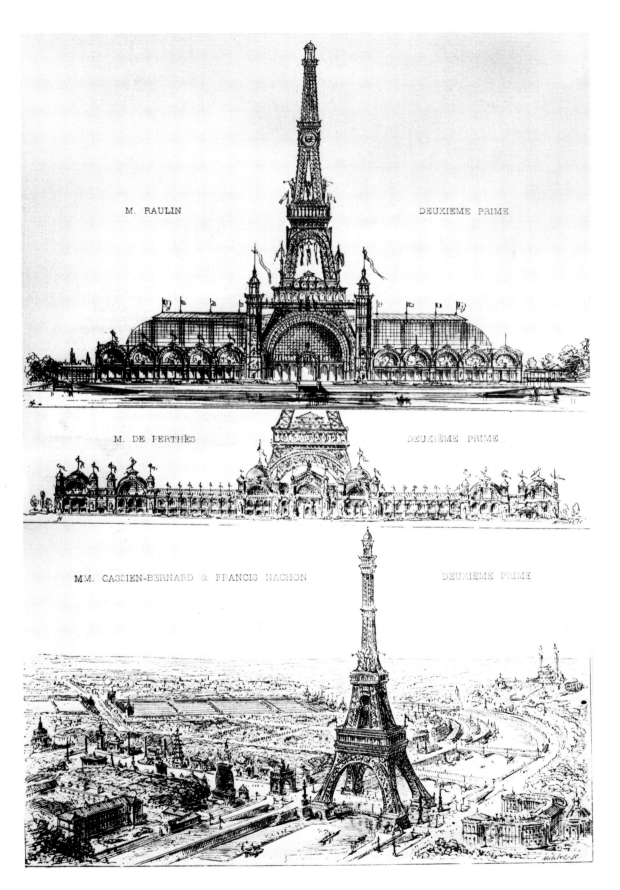

M. RAULIN

DEUXIÈME PRIME

M. DE PERTHÈS

DEUXIÈME PRIME

MM. CASSIEN-BERNARD & FRANCIS NACHON

DEUXIÈME PRIME

TOUR DE 300 MÈTRES

ÉLÉVATION

Échelle de 0ᵐ002 ꝑ 1 Mᵗʳᵉ

Un pour être annexé à notre
Convention en date du 8 Janvier 1887

G. Eiffel

G. EIFFEL.

Ingénieur & Constructeur

Projet dressé avec la collaboration de MM. E. NOUGUIER et M. KOECHLIN, Ingénieurs de la Maison EIFFEL, et S. SAUVESTRE, Architecte

110 300-meter tower, elevation attached to the agreement of January 8, 1887, Paris, Musée d'Orsay, Eiffel collection.

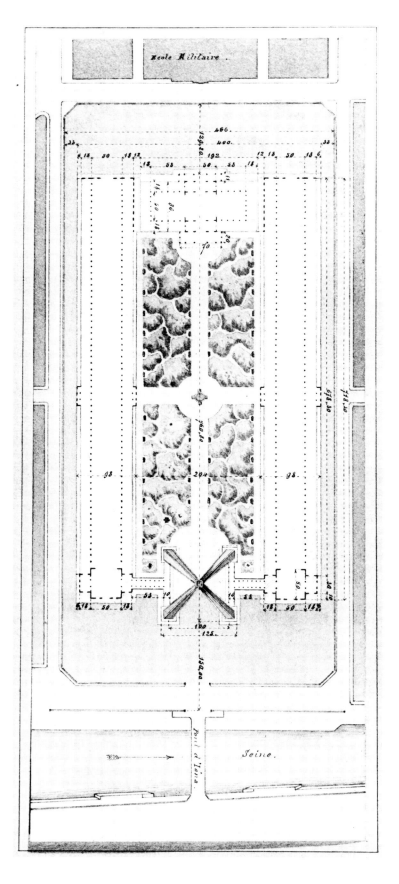

Exhibition by Cassien-Bernard and Francis Nachon, it topped a huge bridge across the Seine which was an extension of the Esplanade des Invalides.

There were serious objections to the Champ de Mars, which Alfred Picard mentions in his report. "Was it sensible to construct the tower in the bottom of the Seine valley? Would it not be better to place it in an elevated position, on a rise which would be a sort of pedestal for it and make it stand out more? Wouldn't the gigantic metal tower overshadow the palaces of the Champ de Mars? Should such a permanent monument be built on the site where future exhibitions would certainly be organized, and thus be forced to include it in the scheme of these exhibitions, when the novelty of the displays is one of the essential elements, if not the principal factor, in their success?"[27]

But to remove the tower from the center of the exhibition and to place it as an annex in some corner of Paris, or even, as some hoped, on the edge of the city, would mean compromising the financial success of the venture. The Eiffel Tower was to be the main attraction of 1889; it was therefore necessary to choose between the Champ de Mars and the Trocadero. The fact that the ground of the Chaillot hill had been excavated to a considerable depth, and that the proximity itself of the 1878 palace involved a certain risk, meant that the Champ de Mars was preferred. A drawing preserved in the French National Archives fixes the final site "approximately halfway between the Trocadero dome and the cupola of the Palace of Various Industries, towards the upper part of the old city gardens, and far enough from the Seine to ensure that the foundations are not too costly."[28]

On January 8, 1887, the agreement allowing work to start was finally signed by Edouard Lockroy, acting for the State, and Eugène Poubelle, Prefect of the Seine department, acting for the City of Paris, on the one hand, and Gustave Eiffel, "acting on his own behalf," on the other. This sixteen-page document, which includes eighteen articles, strictly laid down the time limit for construction, the methods of financing, and the conditions for running the tower.[29] Eiffel, the sole person responsible

111   *Ground plan for the tower on the Champ de Mars*, pen and watercolor, Paris, Archives nationales.

119

since he was acting in his own name and not on behalf of his company, undertook to finish the tower for the opening of the exhibition in 1889, on the site indicated on the attached plan, made over by the State to the City of Paris in 1880. He alone would bear the costs resulting from the construction and running of the tower. "The undertaking shall include the subsoil foundations, the masonry bases, the complete metal carcass, the construction and interior fitting out of the rooms on the levels, and all the lightning conductors and their accessories; but it does not include the layout of the ground within the perimeter of the tower, nor its transformation into avenues, squares, or other arrange-

ments which the Directors of the Exhibition see fit, which will in no case be the responsibility of Monsieur Eiffel." Eiffel's work was to be carried out under the supervision of the exhibition engineers and the special committee set up on May 12, 1886. Article 7 specified the conditions for the financing and running of the tower: "As payment for this work, Monsieur Eiffel shall be granted the sum of one million five hundred thousand francs from the funds allocated to the exhibition, and all income from the commercial exploitation of the tower during the year of the exhibition and the twenty years following, starting from January 1st eighteen hundred and ninety, all under the following conditions:

1) The sum of one million five hundred thousand francs shall be paid as follows: five hundred thousand francs when the metal carcass has

112   *Details of the arch span*, tracing, Paris, Musée d'Orsay, Eiffel collection.

reached the height of the floor of the first platform; five hundred thousand francs when the metal carcass has reached the second platform; five hundred thousand francs when the structure is completed and provisionally accepted for use;

2) During the whole of the exhibition, Monsieur Eiffel shall run the said construction for his own profit and at his own risk, in the manner which he shall judge to be in his best interests, whether by allowing the public to go up or by installing restaurants, cafes, etc.''

Although Eiffel was to decide the admission fees to be charged, the agreement specified maximum charges which were not to be exceeded.

Each level of the tower was to include a room freely available to appropriate bodies, to be used for the performance of scientific or military experiments.

When the exhibition closed, the City of Paris would become the proprietor of the tower, while Eiffel would continue to receive the income from it for twenty years "as an addition to the fee for the work." This allowance of the income from running the tower was extended for seventy years in 1910, but withdrawn in 1980 by the Société Nouvelle d'Exploitation de la Tour Eiffel, in which the City of Paris held a majority.

All that remained to be found was the funding; the grant of 1,500,000 francs would not cover a quarter of the projected costs of 6,500,000. On June 6, 1887, Eiffel was already contemplating the formation of a company with a capital of 5,000,000 francs, divided into ten thousand shares of five hundred francs each. Of these "10,000 founders' portions," half would remain in his possession; "one quarter would be allocated to the issuing company, and the last quarter would be reserved for various parties."[30] When the company was created on December 31, 1888, the two latter quarters were acquired by a consortium of three banks. Even in the event of the most unfavorable conditions (2,550,000 visitors instead of the anticipated 3,056,250, he estimated with remarkable precision), Eiffel declared that "the entire capital can be written off"; but "given the conditions anticipated, the shareholders' capital will be repaid before the end of the exhibition, and their annual dividend, in jouissance shares,* will represent a

---

* Redeemed shares which continue to participate in dividends—Trans.

capital equal to 80 percent of the capital subscribed. The 10,000 founders' shares each have a value of more than 400 francs."[31]

In 1886–87, since Eiffel was still somewhat unsure of the public success of the venture which he had taken on alone, he tried to cover himself, to win contracts which were lucrative and risk free. In a letter of October 14, 1886, to the Director General of Works for the Exhibition, he asked that the construction of the Gallery of Machines be entrusted to him in addition, as a "compensation for all the risks and dangers the construction of the tower means for him, while providing the exhibition with an attraction and success which it would not otherwise have, and which it is getting almost free of charge." This was a legitimate claim, for the risky construction of the tower had obliged him to abandon other projects. What is more, he had been passed over in the competition, and had not received his share of the exhibition work; "not only was Monsieur Eiffel not called upon, he now finds himself banished from the exhibition, pushed to one side."[32] Although his project was presented as being more financially profitable than that of Dutert and Contamin, it was fortunately the latter which was chosen, endowing the Champ de Mars with one of the finest examples of nineteenth-century architecture, until its untoward destruction in 1910.

Work in Progress

Despite Eiffel's laments and his momentary financial doubts, and above all, as we shall see in the next chapter, despite increasing criticism of the project—notably the famous "artists' protest" of February 1887—work began. On January 1, 1887, Eiffel, armed with his concession for the land, took possession of the designated site on the Champ de Mars, which was then still only a vast stretch of sandy ground, an impressive desert in a quarter which had begun to develop since the creation of the twenty-arrondissement Paris in 1860. It was bounded on the west by a few low houses, workshops, and small factories, and on the east by large private houses and wealthier blocks of apartments, whose owners, concerned about the erection of an "industrial" construction on their doorstep, brought a plethora of legal actions against it. The

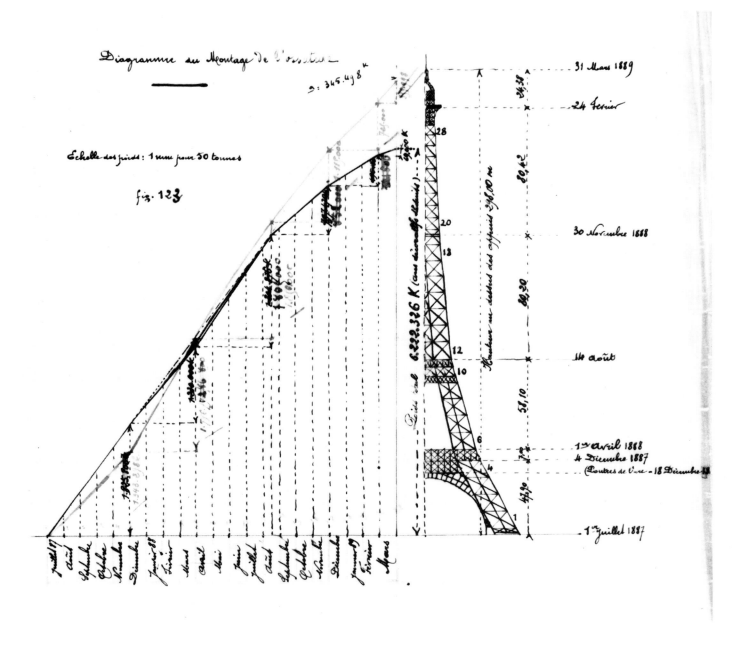

113 *Eiffel Tower*, diagram for the erection of the frame, tracing, Paris, Musée d'Orsay, Eiffel collection.

final project differed slightly from that of 1885 in that it was less "decorated"; the glass-walled hall on the first level was simplified, making it smaller and lower; the ornamental sculptures were removed, as was the intermediate floor which Sauvestre had originally inserted between the second level and the upper platform; in particular, the shape of the four huge arches of the base was changed. In short, the whole construction was given a lighter aspect, with fewer trimmings, more clearly asserting the dominance of the engineer's art over that of the architect. This was a step backwards, a "return to the origins," that is, to the steel pylon originally devised by Nouguier and Koechlin.

The foundation work, which Bourdais had so cavalierly overlooked, was capably carried out by Eiffel. Despite the excellent quality of the subsoil, which was made up of a broad layer of dry, compact clay covered by a good thickness of gravel, the enormous burden of the tower (9 million kilograms) had to be distributed over an area such that the load did not exceed 2 kilograms per square centimeter. As the site was so close to the Seine, a substantial part of it was liable to flooding, and special precautions were taken. "Two systems had to be used: the dry foundation system for the two legs farthest from the river, and the compressed air system for the two nearest the Seine."[33] In May 1887, Eiffel explained his reasons for doing this to the Société des Ingénieurs Civils, of which he was then vice-president. Although the two farthest (the eastern and southern) legs posed no particular problems, since the soil conditions permitted "a perfect foundation with a lower block composed of a 2-meter layer of cement concrete cast in the open air," on the Seine side the mud and marl which lay above the layer of sand and gravel made it necessary to instal piles by means of compressed air using sheet-metal caissons 15 meters long by 6 meters wide, four to each pier, driven in to a

depth of 22 meters, that is, 5 meters below water level. This process was certainly more expensive than using coffer dams and underwater concrete, but it was faster and more reliable.[34]

At the foot of each leg of the tower are four great substructures, each consisting of four distinct foundation blocks (corresponding to the four subpiers of each leg) "laid out along the horizontal projections of the principal arrises, that is, at an angle of 45 degrees to the axis of the Champ de Mars. Each of the blocks comprises, from base to top: (1) a bed of concrete which is 10 meters long, 6 meters wide, and 2 meters thick for the eastern and southern legs, and 15 meters long, 6 meters wide, and 6 meters thick for the northern and western legs; (2) a masonry block made from Souppes stone* in the form of a triangular prism with its vertical surface inwards and inclined surface outwards; the prism's dimensions are such that they bring the oblique resultant of the pressures back to a point very close to the center of the foundations [of each leg]; (3) two courses of Château-Landon ashlar,* intended to support the bearing shoes and normal to the

114 *The Champ de Mars at the beginning of 1887,* with the Trocadero in the background, photograph by Pierre Petit, Paris, Musée d'Orsay, Eiffel collection.

---

* Limestone from the Château-Landon area of north-eastern France—Trans.

115,116 *Preliminary work for the Eiffel Tower foundations,* photographs by Pierre Petit, Paris, Musée d'Orsay, Eiffel collection.

117   *View of the site during the filling of the foundation caissons by the compressed air method,* photograph by Pierre Petit, Paris, Musée d'Orsay, Eiffel collection.

118   *View of the foundation masonry blocks,* built on the compressed air caissons, showing the metal anchorages fixed into the blocks, photograph by Pierre Petit, Paris, Musée d'Orsay, Eiffel collection.

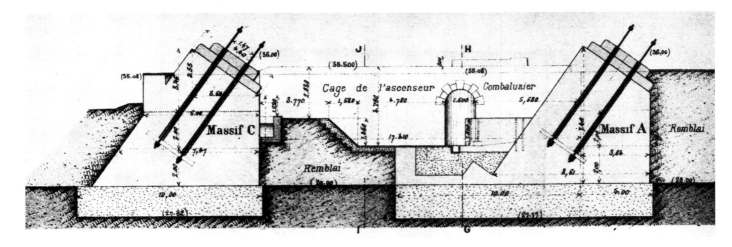

119 *Section through the foundation blocks.*

direction of the ribs." Huge bolts 7.80 meters long sunk into the masonry at the center of all the blocks provide an anchor which is not necessary for the stability of the tower itself, but which was to be used to assemble the legs as cantilevers. Overall the foundations supported loads considerably lower than their maximum resistance. The ordinary masonry bore a load of no more than 4 or 5 kilograms per square centimeter, "while the load on the Château-Landon ashlar, under the shoes, does not exceed 30 kilograms per square centimeter, although the crushing strength of this stone is as high as 1,235 kilograms."[35]

Nevertheless, Eiffel took all eventualities into account. In order to keep the tower's four feet "in a perfectly horizontal plane" whatever happened, he made a cavity in each of the shoes "and installed in each a hydraulic press or jack capable of a force of 800 tonnes." "These presses were to allow the ribs to be shifted and raised by the amount required [...]. When it was necessary, they were used to carry out the exact leveling of all the supports. It was wonderful to regulate the position of such a great mass, just as a surveyor regulates his spirit level with a screw." The foundations, buried in an infill made flush with ground level, were not visible; all that could be seen were the massive bases with their rococo decoration made from masonry blocks "arranged in a picturesque manner," which appeared to support the whole of the metal structure, but which were in fact merely a facing. "The foundations, started on January 28,

1887, were completely finished by June 30 of the same year, the date when construction of the metal part began." During these five months 31,000 cubic meters of ground were excavated, and 12,000 cubic meters of masonry were built up.[36]

Numerous sources enable us to follow the gradual erection of the tower against the Parisian sky. In addition to the bibliographical sources which have regularly been referred to (of which the most detailed is Eiffel's own monumental work, *La Tour de 300 mètres*, published on the occasion of the Universal Exhibition in 1900, the most concise the *Rapport* written by Alfred Picard after the 1889 Exhibition), there are the many photographic studies which were inevitably made of this strange construction, including a vast album compiled by Durandelle, probably at Eiffel's own request, which contains a valuable series of photographs taken from the same vantage point; photographs by Petit; astonishing pictures taken by an anonymous visitor when construction work was almost complete; as well as prints and paintings (notably those by Seurat). Whereas the progress of such large constructions as the Garabit viaduct had been followed and commented on only by a few specialists, the work on the tower was observed daily by a crowd of passersby: "We saw them exca-

Pages 127–136
120–138 *Photographs of the Eiffel Tower under construction,* taken from the same viewpoint, the east tower of the Trocadero (August 1887–April 1889), Paris, Musée d'Orsay, Eiffel collection.

10 Août 1887

9 Septembre 1887

8 Octobre 1887   10 Novembre 1887.

14 Decembre 1887

15 Mars 1888

10 Avril 1888

10 Mai 1888

Juin 1888

Juillet 188

14 Aout 1888   14 Septembre 1888

14 Octobre 1888

14 Novembre 1888

26 Décembre 1888

20 Janvier 1889

12 Février 1889

12 Mars 1889

2 Avril 1889

139   *State of the work, June 30, 1887*, photograph by Durandelle, Paris, Musée d'Orsay, Eiffel collection.

140   *State of the work, July 18, 1887*, photograph by Durandelle, Paris, Musée d'Orsay, Eiffel collection.

vate these foundations with the aid of compressed-air caissons, in the deep clay where the first inhabitants of Grenelle* hunted reindeer and wild oxen," observed the well-disposed Vicomte de Vogüé. "Soon the elephant's four megalithic feet weighed down upon the ground; the principal members sprang forward as cantilevers from the stone shoes, overturning all our ideas about the stability of a construction."[37]

The mathematical growth of this metal tower was a new and unexpected spectacle. To begin with, using only hoisting gins, the sections of the legs were placed end to end, immediately drifted,

* Former village on the Seine which became part of the fifteenth arrondissement in 1860—Trans.

and then bolted. "Then came the trusses and struts which, by joining together the parts of the leg which had already been put up, corrected their relative positions and braced them at the same time by forming an indeformable whole. The assembly teams were followed by teams of riveters who replaced the bolts with heat-sunk rivets which formed the real, final bond between the different components."[38]

Above a height of 15 meters, however, the ordinary hoisting gins had to be replaced by four cranes, each weighing 12,000 kilograms, which were specially constructed according to a plan drawn up by Eiffel. "These were pivoting cranes; they had a reach of 12 meters, which allowed them

to serve each of the four uprights of the pier and all intermediate points, and they had a strength of 4,000 kilograms. They were supported only by the sections already in place, and they made their way gradually along the elevator girders, as the superstructure was erected."[39]

Using this system, it was possible to construct the inclined legs to a height of 30 meters as if they had been vertical piers; subsequently twelve pyramidal wooden scaffolds had to be installed, "set up so that their tops supported the three interior ribs of each leg."[40] Seen from the ground, the system appeared hazardous, and lifting material a difficult operation: "cranes clung onto the uprights; they clambered along the girders like crabs with enormous pincers; they took items from the ground and bore them away to distribute them up above, sending them flying off in every direction."[41] In fact, the control was very exact, and, as if replying to this astonished layman, the man of science explains

141, 142 *State of the work in September 1887*, photographs by Pierre Petit, Paris, Musée d'Orsay, Eiffel collection.

143 *Worksite seen from the first platform*, January 14, 1888, ▷ photograph by Durandelle, Paris, Musée d'Orsay, Eiffel collection.

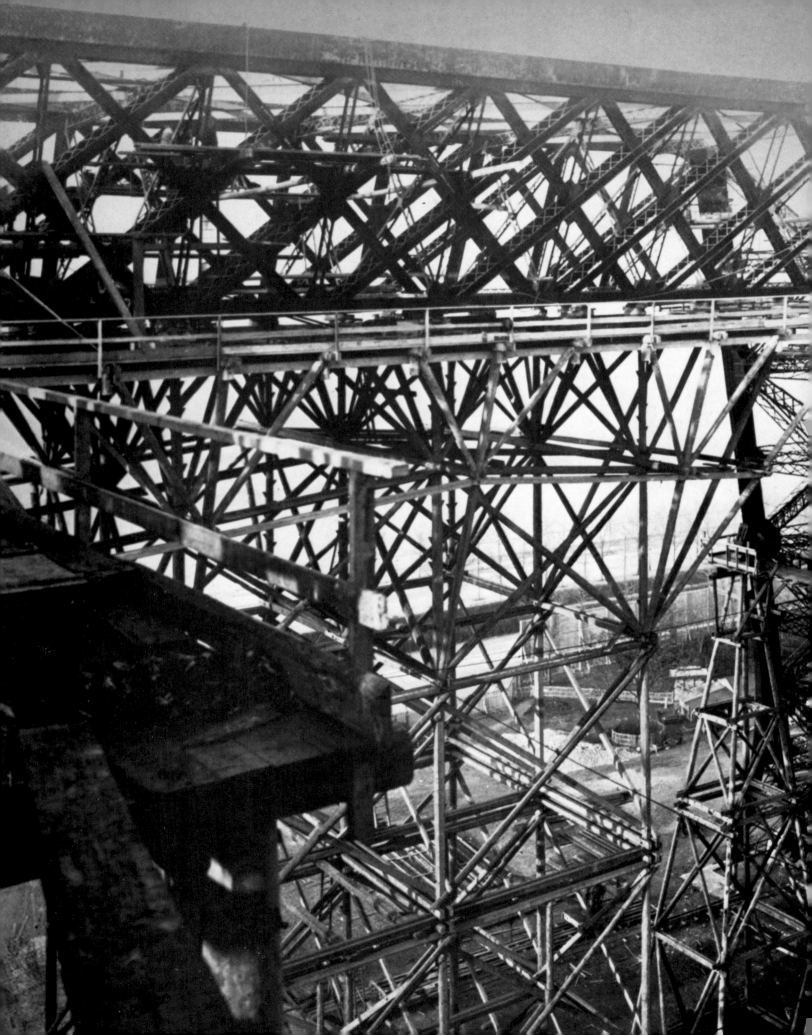

that "each of the ribs was supported on the upper platform of its pylon by means of horizontal-topped falsework resting on boxes of sand like those used for striking the centering from bridges. Extremely precise adjustment of the position of the elements was very simple. If the pier needed to be inclined slightly, it was sufficient to drain the required quantity of sand from the boxes, and the falsework would move into position. If, on the other hand, the pier was to be lifted, the falsework had simply to be moved by means of hydraulic jacks supported by the upper platform of the pylons."[42]

Above the height of 55 meters, new 45-meter long vertical scaffolds had to be built to provide a stage 25 meters long for each side of the tower. The metal members were hoisted onto these platforms and then assembled as cantilevers so as to connect adjoining piers. In this way the four beams forming the first platform of the tower were placed in position (March 15, 1888). The cranes which had been used in the construction of the first platform then enabled work up to the second to be continued without difficulty. In order to save time and to ensure that the machinery described above was not the only lifting equipment available, Eiffel arranged a crane driven by a 10-horsepower transportable engine on the floor of the first level; "this

144 *The tower at first platform level,* January 1888, photograph, Paris, Musée d'Orsay, Eiffel collection.

145 *Constructional detail of one metal leg,* photograph, Paris, ▷ Musée d'Orsay, Eiffel collection.

146   *State of the work in mid-March 1888*, photograph, Paris, Musée d'Orsay, Eiffel collection.

147   *State of the work in May 1888*, photograph, Paris, Musée d'Orsay, Eiffel collection.

148   *State of the work in October 1888*, photograph, Paris, ▷ Musée d'Orsay, Eiffel collection.

crane took components from the ground, lifted them up to the first platform, and placed them in small wagons which then traveled around a circular track to the required point, where the parts were taken up by the cranes on the struts."[43] Using this system, it was possible to complete the second platform by July 1888.

For the last phase of construction, Eiffel had to make slight changes to the construction method used hitherto. Between the second level and the top, there were no more inclined paths for the construction machinery to travel along, and it could only be supported by the vertical column formed by the central guide rail for the elevators. With the addition of 3-meter-high frames onto which the supports of the cranes could easily be bolted, each crane being "fixed onto both sides of the central elevator shaft so that they were balanced,"[44] the same reliable, rapid, and efficient system of construction could be used. From then on, "the slender column moved swiftly up into space";[45] little could be seen from the ground any longer since "the autumn mists often veiled the airy construction site."[46] On March 31, 1889, construction was finished and the tricolor was hoisted at the top of the lightning conductor.

149 *"Sectional drawing of the metal framework,"* plate from G. Eiffel, *La Tour de 300 mètres*, Paris, 1900.

150 *Detail of the upper part of the tower and the beacon*, plate ▷ from G. Eiffel, *La Tour de 300 mètres*, Paris, 1900.

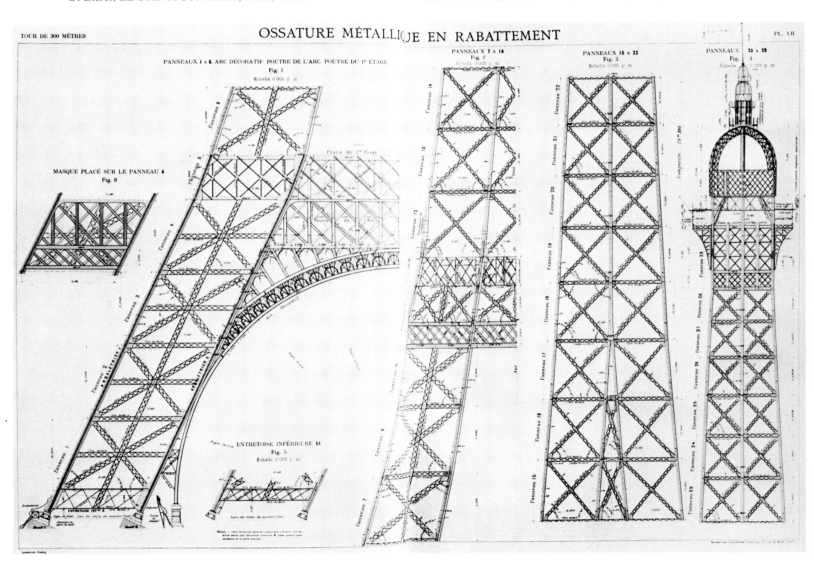

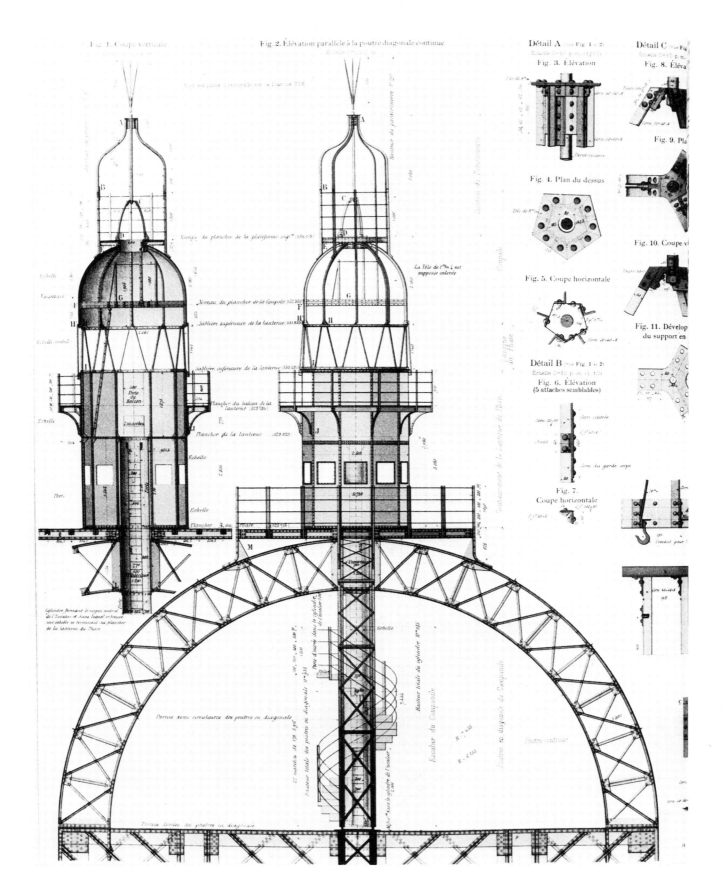

147

Behind the Scenes

"The construction of the tower does Monsieur Eiffel and his associates great honor. It was organized and conducted with rare talent, and may be cited as a model of order, simplicity, ingeniousness, precision, speed, and safety."[47] Yet no one could be more complimentary than Alfred Picard in his *Rapport;* and although it is true that Gustave Eiffel had no hand in the design of the 300-meter tower, only he could have carried out such a venture.

All too often attention is focused on what was happening on the Champ de Mars; the backstage work is overlooked—all the preparations in the Levallois-Perret workshops which made the mathematical progress of the tower possible. Only with the perfect organization of the drawing office under Maurice Koechlin, who made 1,700 general drawings for the skeleton of the tower alone, and of the detailed drawings supervised by Pluot, who made 3,629, showing 18,038 different parts, could such strictly regulated progress take place.

However, two problems rendered the design work laborious. The first was the fineness of the working drawings, for "the assembled parts were always in oblique planes at varying angles, and, furthermore, they were almost all different from one another."[48] The second problem concerned the working method which Eiffel had previously introduced, "to which we kept more strictly than ever," he says, "in view of the particular difficulties of this construction." At Levallois each individual part was drawn "and the position of the different rivet holes by which it would be joined to the adjacent parts was calculated with an exactness which required the constant use of logarithms. The distances between all the rivet holes were calculated to within one tenth of a millimeter. Each part therefore required specific study and its own drawing, which was usually made on a scale of 1:2 for the smaller parts and 1:5 for the larger."[49]

This system was the opposite of that used for the great engineering works in Britain, even for a structure as large and important as the Forth Bridge. "Using our method, all the holes were drilled extremely accurately in advance, assembly was regulated by the holes themselves, and parts were brought into their exact assembly position by drifting, that is, by driving a large number of tapered steel pins into the holes." In most cases no check

was needed and construction on the Champ de Mars progressed as it had been planned in the workshops. "Thus the different parts were completely and thoroughly prepared off the site, and on site they were simply placed in position and carefully fixed to one another."[50] This perfect organization, which won Eiffel universal praise, gave all observers the impression that the tower was constructing itself, like a Meccano set; it was a smooth, well-oiled operation where human participation seemed limited, almost nonexistent.

Indeed, Alfred Picard confirms this: "Despite the extent of the construction work, the large number of work teams which might have been expected were not to be seen on the site."[51] There were never more than 250 workers, of whom 199 were permanent, and whose names were engraved on the tower, and listed reverently by Barral in his *Panthéon scientifique.* "It is thus a historical document," he explains, "and reproducing their names in this book will make it a sort of certificate of honor for the families of these proud workmen."[52] From Alézy to Zettelmaier, they are all there, in alphabetical order, sometimes with their job added (head barrowman, head carpenter, painting supervisor, masonry supervisor, foreman, etc.) or their relationship specified (Braley [father] and Braley [eldest son]; Calmels Sr. and Calmels Jr.). "All of them vied with one another in zeal, and they all devoted themselves totally to the common task, flagging neither from tiredness nor in bad weather, working in mid-winter as they did on the hottest days, taking on all obstacles with complete confidence and a firm desire to achieve the goal."[53] There was only one death and one widow discreetly compensated, and the construction workers' wages increased as the tower grew, to "reward them for their devotion and courage."[54] This is how the social history of the construction of the tower is generally summed up.

It must nevertheless be pointed out that the working day was twelve hours in the summer months, ten or eleven hours in spring and autumn, and nine hours in winter; "and in May 1889, exceptionally, they worked thirteen hours per day." The hourly pay increased substantially between June 1888 and December of the same year, but did not change again before the opening of the tower. In June 1888, a carpenter, the highest-paid worker, earned 0.70 francs per hour; in December, 0.95 francs; during the same period the hourly rate for construction workers and riveters increased from 0.60 to 0.85 francs.[55]

The installation of a canteen on the first platform, then almost finished, in February or March 1888, was not only a social move (the food, which was of "strictly supervised" quality, cost 20 percent less than ordinary prices, the difference being paid back to the canteen manager by the construction site office); it was also a clever calculation, for "this additional expense, which was borne by the company, was recouped, as the time loss due to workers going down and back up again, and their resulting tiredness from this, were eliminated."[56]

This concern for workers' welfare did not prevent a sporadic strike movement in September and December 1888. Eiffel, who had already agreed to pay the automatic 2 percent deduction from wages for accident insurance, and considered this "encouragement" quite sufficient, was confronted, from the spring of 1888 on, by "a request for an increase in the daily wage rates which had operated up to that point." He refused, insisting that "for a true construction worker vertigo does not exist," and that the growth of the tower did not make the work any more dangerous. "The professional risks remained the same; whether a man fell from 40 meters or 300 meters, the result was the same—certain death."[57]

The logic of this reasoning did little to convince his employees, who stopped work for three days on September 19, and won a progressive increase of "0.05 francs each month, up to a maximum of 0.20 francs." Work restarted without incident; but when the intermediate level was reached on December 20, that is, the time when the progressive monthly increase agreed on September 20 was about to reach its maximum, new demands were made, and there was another strike. Eiffel did not want to give in, for he feared that he would compromise the entire project by repeated concessions, and above all refused to give his workers "the idea that they were indispensable to the smooth running of the work." "To show them that I was guided far less by financial considerations than by my wish to see the success of the work begun," he explained, "I promised that a bonus of 100 francs would be granted to all construction workers who continued working until the flag was raised. Furthermore, I declared that all those who were not present at midday the following day would be dismissed and replaced by new workers."

The large majority accepted, and those who left were immediately replaced by "newcomers who went up to 200 meters straightway, and after half a day were able to perform the same tasks as the old ones." "Thus," Eiffel concluded, "it was proved that with the proper equipment a good construction worker can work at any height without feeling unwell." Rather than sacking the ringleaders, Eiffel restricted them to putting up the arches on the first level, forbidding them to go above this level under threat of dismissal—a clever move which humiliated them in front of those who were "in the front line" of construction. "Their workmates laughed at them, calling them the indispensables, and soon afterwards they left."[58]

The last important part of the construction was the installation of the elevators. They served the tower's three platforms, backed up by staircases which enabled the public to climb to the second level (the staircase from the second to the third level was only for servicing). The west staircase, reserved for the ascent, could accommodate 2,000 to 2,500 people every hour.

The following elevator machinery was provided:

> From the ground to the first platform, two elevators made by Roux, Combaluzier, and Lepape, placed in the east and west legs;
> From the ground to the second platform (direct journey) an Otis elevator placed in the north leg;
> From the first platform to the second, a second Otis elevator placed in the south leg;
> From the second to the third platform, an Edoux elevator.[59]

The construction of the elevators was complicated by the inclination of the legs of the tower, which varied from 54° at the base to 80° at the second platform, and by the difficulty of achieving a vertical ascent of 160.20 meters from this second platform.

In the elevators in the east and west legs, the cars are driven by two endless chains made of a series of interconnecting articulated rods. Each car consists of two compartments one on top of the other, with four rollers which enable it to move on "a track fixed to the girders of the elevator shaft,"[60] and could carry one hundred passengers (seventy standing and thirty seated). Although the journey up to the first platform took only one minute, the number of return journeys of the car was limited to ten per hour, thus giving an hourly rate of two thousand passengers for the two elevators.

The system installed in the north leg, devised by the American firm Otis, is different. The car is driven by "a tackle connected to a hydraulic plunger. A cast-iron cylinder 0.95 meters in diameter and about 11 meters long was placed in the foot of the tower parallel to the principal members. A plunger, activated by water drawn from reservoirs set up on the second level, and consequently at a pressure of 11 to 12 atmospheres, moves in this cylinder. The rod of the plunger operates a carriage carrying six moving pulleys of 1.50-meter diameter, and each of these pulleys corresponds to a fixed pulley of the same diameter, thus forming an enormous block and tackle with twelve sides of cable. The fall of this huge tackle passes over guide pulleys placed at intervals up to a point above the second level, and comes back down and is attached to the car. In this way for every one meter the plunger moves in the cylinder, the car moves 12 meters up or down." As in the French system, the car consisted of two compartments one on top of the other. "They can only hold forty people, as it was considered that all the passengers should be seated, in view of the change in the inclination of the piers between the first and second platforms."[61]

The Edoux type of elevator, "a car driven by a hydraulic plunger operated by pressurized water," had already been used in the Trocadero, but had been substantially improved since 1878. "Instead of attempting the extremely difficult task of covering the 160 meters separating the second and third platforms in one journey, this height was divided into two stages by means of an intermediate landing placed 80 meters above the second platform. The lower stage is served by a car which acts as a counterweight to the first car and is connected to it by cables; when the counterweight is at the level of the second platform, the elevator is at the top of its run; when the counterweight goes up, the elevator comes down, and the two come together at the intermediate landing, where the passengers are transferred from one car into the other."[62]

The elevator had become widely used since its first introduction at the Universal Exhibition of 1867; it had been continuously improved and decorated—it was to be the subject of a competi-

tion at the Ecole des Beaux-Arts—and for the Eiffel Tower it became an essential piece of equipment. The various systems installed in 1889 engaged the commentators' attention to a considerable degree; in his *Rapport*, Alfred Picard devoted to them a fifth of the chapter on Eiffel's monumental work. And there is no doubt that their ingenious design and faultless efficiency merited these long descriptions. "To sum up," Eiffel himself remarked in the visitors' guide he wrote later, "this very complex, intricate problem, full of danger and uncertainty, was solved to the great glory of French industry. They ensure complete safety for visitors, and their rapid, accurate, and mathematical operation up to such great heights is one of the chief points of interest, not to say one of the great pleasures for visitors to the 300-meter tower."[63]

Through Visitors' Eyes

"When we arrived in Paris, our first idea was to go and see the tower—I don't need to tell you which tower, do I?—And of course, the merry band wanted to go up as high as they could, no more and no less than Madame Malb'rough. During the journey we talked of nothing else; the children could not sleep for thinking about it." That is how Eugène Reboul introduced his little volume *Souvenir de mon ascension à la Tour Eiffel*, written conscientiously in August 1888, and sold from the first days when the tower was opened to the public.[64] The visitor chooses the level he wishes to go to and buys a ticket for it; he enters an "extremely elegant" car, "fitted with very comfortable seats all round"; but this is after standing in line for three-quarters of an hour to an hour, for the elevators were crowded out. "Now we have settled ourselves in. A trumpet, bugle, or horn blows or whistles; we are off. Up above two huge wheels, lost in the entanglement of the tower, turn slowly and heavily, chanting 'clang-clang, clang-clang'; the ropes stretch out and pull back, other, relatively small wheels turn without haste, and the great snail

151 Georges Garen, *Illumination of the Eiffel Tower during the 1889 Universal Exhibition*, engraving, Paris, Musée d'Orsay, Eiffel collection.

LA TOUR EIFFEL ET LES PLUS HAUTS MONUMENTS DU GLOBE

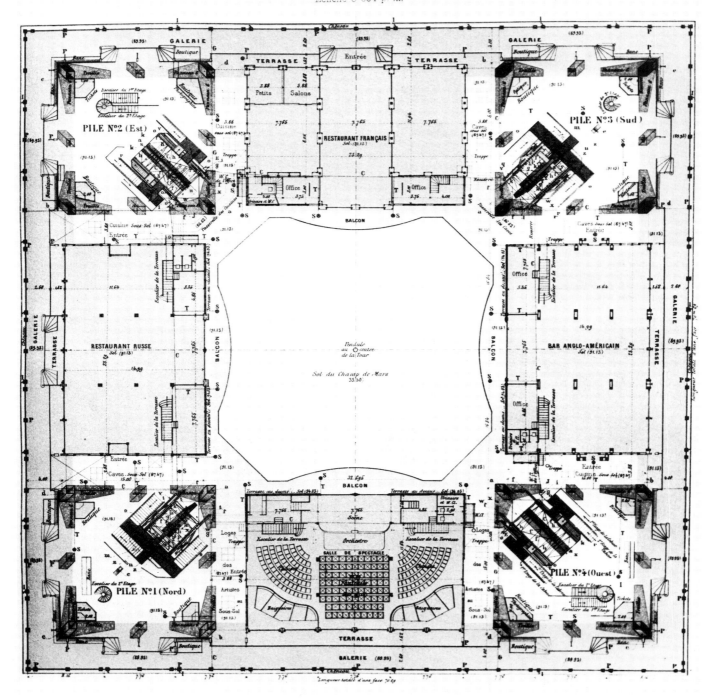

AMÉNAGEMENT DU PREMIER ÉTAGE
Fig. 3. Coupe horizontale
Échelle 0ᵐ004 p. m.

152 *"The Eiffel Tower and the highest monuments in the world,"* engraving published in the *Revue illustrée*, 1889.

153 *Plan of the first platform*, plate from G. Eiffel, *La Tour de 300 mètres*, Paris, 1900.

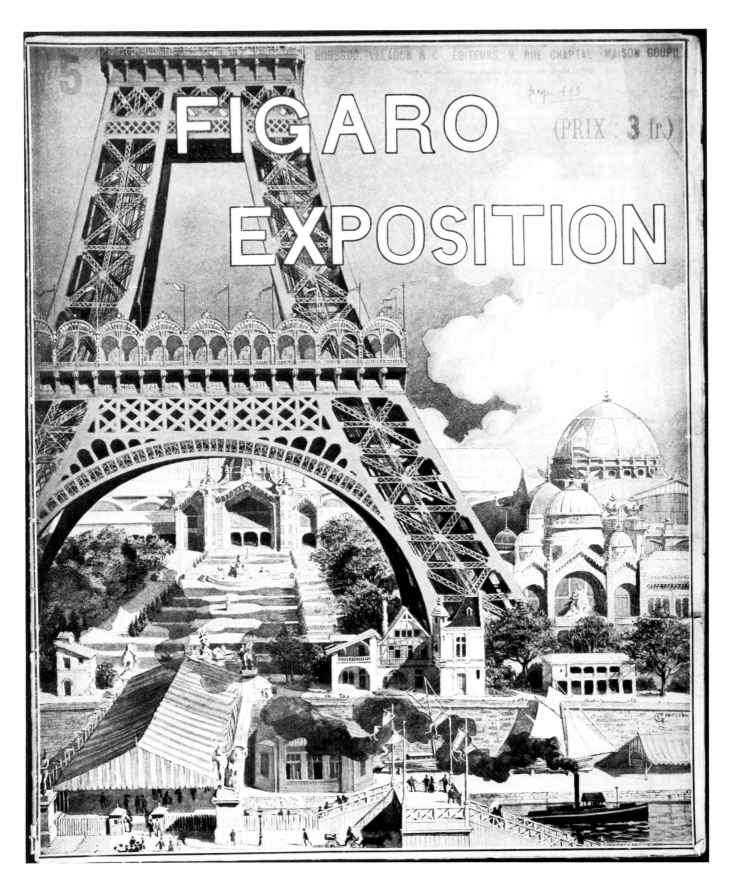

◁ 154 Cover for the Figaro Exposition, 1889, with the Eiffel Tower and, at its feet, some of the houses from Charles Garnier's *Histoire de l'habitation humaine.*

155 *"M. Eiffel's rooms on the fourth platform (285 meters from the ground),"* before 1914, photograph published in the *Souvenir de la Tour Eiffel*, Paris, 1900.

moves upwards, with you sitting in its belly— unless you are in its head, for it has two floors, two cavities, two stomachs, this wooden beast with iron wheels for feet, which shudders like an animal under the hand of the operator who tames it."[65] Outside, on a vertical rod which goes all the way up the elevator shaft, the heights reached are marked, from meter to meter; there are also very legible markers, white on blue, enabling the passengers "to compare the height they have reached to that of the best-known monuments, or the tops of structures surrounding us":[66] 20 meters was the strictly controlled maximum height of houses in the new Paris; 43 meters was the height of the column in the Place Vendôme; 46 meters, Bartholdi's Statue of Liberty; 66 meters, the towers of Notre-Dame; 110, the dome of Saint Paul's in London; 128, the Garabit viaduct; at 170 meters "we finally overtake the highest monument in the world, the great obelisk in Washington, which is only 169.25 meters high; it is made of masonry, and is extremely ugly from top to bottom."[67]

On the first platform, a French restaurant, a Russian restaurant, an Anglo-American bar, and a 250-seat theater were installed round the central space; this was the "land of eating and drinking," where "each construction is of a style which reflects its name,"[68] exhibition architecture in the worst sense of the term, like that of most of the pavilions scattered between the Champ de Mars and the Trocadero. Next to these constructions there were tobacconists' stalls, women hiring out binoculars, and the inevitable souvenir sellers, "a whole spa town street transported aloft, among the yards, topmasts, and mizzens of a sailing ship with no sails."[69]

On the second level were the printing office of the *Figaro* newspaper, set up there for the duration of the exhibition, the bakeshop, the refreshment stall, and the helicoidal staircase, inaccessible to the public, with its fine spiral banister rail "like a serpent coiling and fleeing around a giant coconut palm." After taking the Edoux elevator and changing cars halfway, the visitor finally reached the last platform; "one is not allowed to go any higher; but there are 'open sesames.' So here is a little spiral staircase, there is a circular hall with rooms opening off it; one of these is reserved for Monsieur Eiffel, the others are laboratories. These rooms overlook a terrace outside, on which a little railroad runs, carrying round the electric spotlights at night."[70] This is at the height of 280 meters; a final spiral staircase gives access to the lamp room, topped by the tricolor.

In 1855, Napoleon III, no doubt wishing to retain a reminder of his capital as it was before Haussmann's great works, had commissioned the painter Navlet to execute a huge panoramic view of Paris from a balloon.[71] Thirty-five years later, the tower enabled everyone to take in the city, to have, in a few minutes, a swift view from the Bois de Boulogne to Vincennes, from Saint-Denis to Montrouge, and even further. One unreserved enthusiast for Eiffel's work seriously claimed that with a telescope it was possible to read a shop sign in Pontoise. A "special map of the environs of Paris, showing the places which can be seen from the top of the Eiffel Tower," was drawn up by the director of the tower's Optical Department, Raoul d'Esclaibes d'Hust, and published as an appendix to Eiffel's work *La Tour en 1900;* it claimed to prove that on a clear day it was possible to see as far as Evreux, Provins, Château-Thierry, and beyond Chartres and Beauvais. But although people could see a long way, it was above all the well-known monuments which stood out above the

rest in the bird's-eye view. One could also comprehend the gradual urbanization of those western quarters of the city which the tower overshadowed, the regular plan of the streets, the harsh lines of gray housefronts, while here and there a church or the green splash of a public garden showed through. This was a new spectacle which went against all the predictions. No, we don't get vertigo; no, it doesn't seem as if all movement has stopped. On the contrary, "life down there" speeds up; "the people walking seem to be running, throwing their legs forward like robots."[72]

It was above all in the evening that, as all observers agreed, the view became "without its equal in the world."[73] Eugène-Melchior de Vogüé, who, while he admired this triumph of engineering, pondered the emptiness of science, has left us with the most beautiful—and the least known—of the descriptions of this view: "I had remained alone in the glass room, just like the poop of a ship, with its chains, capstans, and its electric lamps hanging from the low ceiling. To complete the illusion, the

156 *The Pantheon seen from the fourth platform,* "photograph taken by a lens with a one-meter focal length at one hundredth of a second" (negative by Captain Bouttieaux), published in G. Eiffel, *La Tour Eiffel en 1900*, Paris, 1902.

157   Albert Londe, *Nine photographs taken during a visit to the tower with Gustave Eiffel*, Paris, Musée d'Orsay, Eiffel collection.

158 *Gustave Eiffel and his son-in-law Adolphe Salles on the tower*, 1889.

wind was raging that night in the metal tackle. Its lament was all that could be heard in the silence, and occasionally the ringing of the telephone, calling the lamp look-out above my head. Only the Ocean below was missing. There was Paris. The sun was sinking behind Mont-Valérien.... Night fell; or rather, from the sky which was still light at this height, I could see the crepe veils thickening and rising from below; it seemed as if night was being drawn up from Paris. The quarters of the city faded away one by one ... a few lights were lit, and soon there was an infinite number of them; myriad lights filled the depths of this abyss, making strange constellations, joining with those of the celestial vault at the horizon. It looked like the sky turned upside down, continuing the other one, with an even greater wealth of stars.... Suddenly two bars of light fell on the ground. These were the great beams coming from the spotlights which were moving round above my head: the rays of which we see some fragment each evening, playing in front of our windows, in a little corner of the sky, like the glint of lightning tamed. Seen from their source, the two arms of light seemed to feel their way in the night, with jerky, uncoordinated movements, with feverish constraints which spread them out into a fan or pressed them together like a pencil; you would have sworn that they were looking directionlessly for something lost, or striving to seize some elusive object in space. They were searching Paris at random. Now and then they came together to light up the spot they were examining more brightly. They rested successively

159 *View of the 1889 Universal Exhibition, the Trocadero and the Champ de Mars*, engraving, Paris, Musée d'Orsay, Eiffel collection.

Albert Edward P.

Prince de Galles, devenu depuis Roi d'Angleterre sous le nom d'Edouard VII.

June 10/89.

Alexandra Princess of Wales —

June 10th 1889.

George.

devenu, depuis, Roi d'Angleterre, sous le nom de George V.

Victoria.

Maud.

devenue, depuis, Reine de Norvège.

S. M. Le Roi Edouard VII, alors Prince de Galles, et Sa famille ont fait les premiers, le 10 Juin 89, l'ascension de la Tour jusqu'au sommet.

G. Eiffel

160 *First page of the "Livre d'Or de la Tour Eiffel,"* bearing the signature of various members of the English royal family and Eiffel's handwritten endorsement: "His Majesty King Edward VII, then Prince of Wales, and his family were the first to ascend to the top of the Tower, June 10, 1889," Paris, Musée d'Orsay, Eiffel collection.

161 Stephen Sauvestre, *Plan for the conversion of the Eiffel Tower for the 1900 Universal Exhibition,* 1896, pen and watercolor, Paris, S.N.T.E.

on humble houses, on palaces, and on the distant countryside. I could not weary of following their search, so deliberate and anxious it seemed."[74]

Over the duration of the exhibition, 1,953,122 people visited the tower; over seven months, from May 15 to November 6, this meant an average of 11,800 visitors per day. On the one day of Monday June 10 (Whit Monday), there were 23,202 visitors. "On Mondays through Saturdays the charge was 2 francs for the first level, 3 francs for the second, and 5 francs for the third. These figures were reduced to 1 franc, 1.50 francs, and 2 francs respectively on Sunday between 11 o'clock in the morning and 6 o'clock in the evening. Visitors were allowed to use the stairs or the elevators as they wished between the ground and the second platform, with no extra

162   H. Toussaint, *Plan for the conversion of the Eiffel Tower into a Palace of Electricity and Engineering for the 1900 Universal Exhibition*, elevation, pen, gouache and watercolor, Paris, Musée d'Orsay, Eiffel collection.

charge for the elevators."[75] Receipts therefore totaled 6,509,901 francs 80 centimes, as against a total construction cost of 7,457,000 francs. The million francs' difference was quickly made up after the exhibition closed.

163   H. Toussaint, *Plan for the conversion of the Eiffel Tower into a Palace of Electricity and Engineering for the 1900 Universal Exhibition*, cross section, gouache and watercolor, Paris, Musée d'Orsay, Eiffel collection.

The Tower as a Subject of Controversy

The undeniable success of the tower as an attraction, which made it a profitable operation, nevertheless did nothing to disarm its opponents. So, for the Universal Exhibition of 1900, it was systematically "dressed up" in all the plans presented for the competition; it escaped unscathed thanks to an agreement made on December 28, 1897 between the authorities and the Tower Company.

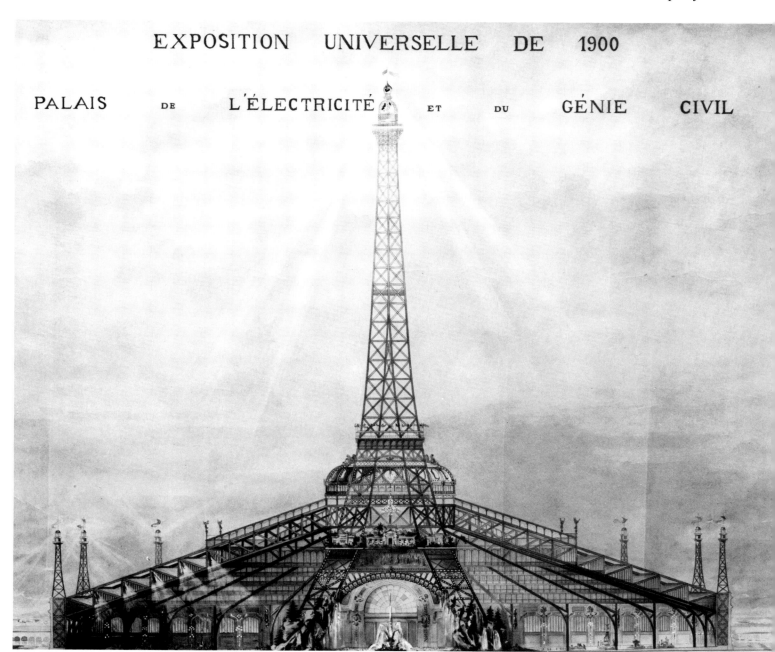

EXPOSITION   UNIVERSELLE   DE   1900

PALAIS   DE   L'ÉLECTRICITÉ   ET   DU   GÉNIE   CIVIL

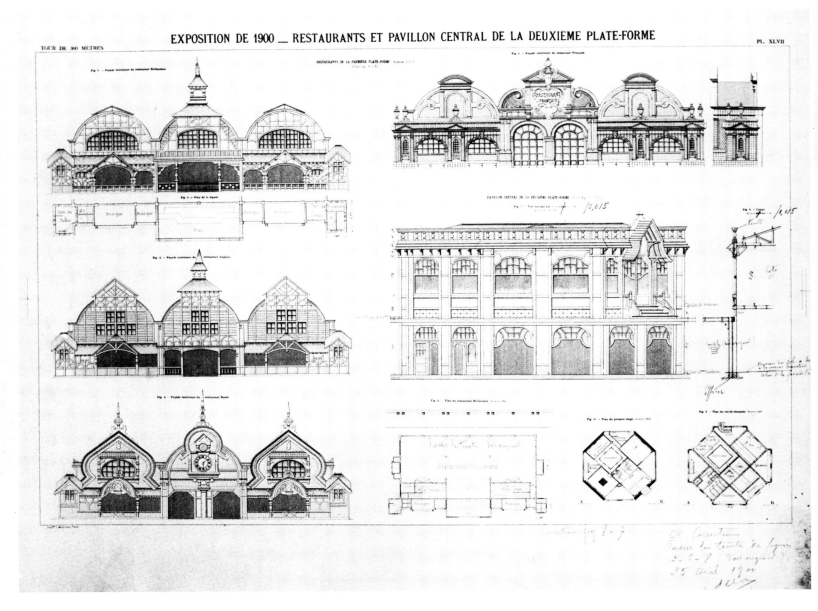

164 *"1900 Exhibition. Restaurants and central pavilion on the second platform,"* plate from G. Eiffel, *La Tour de 300 mètres*, Paris, 1900.

165 *General View of the 1900 Universal Exhibition*, engraving, Paris, Musée d'Orsay, Eiffel collection. ▷

166 André Granet, *The Eiffel Tower Illuminated for the 1937 Exhibition*, gouache, Paris, Musée d'Orsay, Eiffel collection. ▷

According to this, it was integrated into the exhibition and Eiffel was obliged to illuminate it with electric light at night. New arrangements were supposed to result in a better "return," but the public stayed away. By 1900, the tower was no longer a novelty. "The general conditions of operation in comparison with 1889 have changed considerably," Eiffel lamented, "as a result of circum-stances which it is useless to dwell on, such as the excessive size of the exhibition, and the exaggerated number of attractions offered to the public, which came to ruin almost without exception. The number of hours of full-time operation was very limited; the Champ de Mars was almost deserted until two in the afternoon, whereas during the 1889 exhibition the lines of passengers for the elevators

began to form as early as nine o'clock in the morning and did not finish until sunset."[76] In 1900, 1,017,281 visitors went up the tower—51 percent fewer than in 1889.

In an exhibition where "nature and logic are distorted for the sake of distortion,"[77] and where metal was carefully concealed in many constructions, such as the Grand Palais and the Gare d'Or-

say, the Eiffel Tower was henceforth an anachronism; it was dated. What was to save it, apart from clauses in the contract, was its indisputable utility. Since 1889, Eiffel had been carrying out a large number of experiments in optics, communications, meteorology, and aerodynamics. In 1903, the Association française pour l'avancement des Sciences was once again obliged to produce a *Protestation contre la proposition de démolition de la Tour Eiffel;* the Société d'Ingénieurs Civils followed suit.[78]

A highly authoritative report by Jean-Louis Pascal, architect, pupil of Charles Garnier, and a member of the Institut de France, was presented to the Seine Prefect at the point when further continuation of the concession was under discussion; it clearly highlights the divergence of opinion: "It is certainly true that the huge leg span of the tower

cuts the long view which could be seen from the Trocadero to the Ecole Militaire, but, apart from the fact that in itself it presents a very exceptional and unusual appearance, however debatable the form of this daring construction may be, beyond its great plunge into the ground, and between its huge arches, there remains a distance long enough to be able to enjoy a view which is still extensive."[79] However, according to the opponents of the tower, "all the effect which could be gained from uniting the Champ de Mars with the Trocadero Palace in a single great whole is lost."

Those in favor of conserving the tower won the day after fierce debates, thanks to the support of Pascal and Trélat, and in spite of the opposition of Daumet, Lisch, and, of course, the acrimonious Bourdais. Although in favor of keeping the tower, Pascal's somewhat lukewarm conclusions show clearly that, at the turn of the century, there were very few who would defend the tower's aesthetic quality: "the value of a construction which is, after all, unique in the world; the scientific and practical solution to this problem which is as new as it was on its first day; the constantly maintained curiosity of the visitors who return filled with wonder at the panoramic view from 300 meters; and, above all, the exceptional suitability of this building for past, present, and future scientific research, especially for meteorological observations, for which no

other building offers the same resources. Should all this be sacrificed to a harsh aesthetic evaluation, and should this colossal building be destroyed, perhaps at great expense, with no compensation for the city? It would certainly be better if it had been built on a hill rather than in a valley, and one could wish it were more beautiful, but it is used for optical telegraphy, it makes an excellent reference point for the work on the Trocadero lamps, and it can be used for a thousand other purposes. If it did not exist, one would probably not contemplate building it there, or even perhaps anywhere else; but it does exist. Do you not think that the world would be astonished to see us destroy something in our city which continues to be a subject of astonishment for others?"[80] The world was not to be astonished, but the neighboring Gallery of Machines was pulled down seven years later.

What is being questioned in Pascal's fascinating text is once again, as ever, the place of an "industrial" construction in Paris; what is put in question is yet again the distinctive beauty of engineering structures. An old debate which had opened fifty years earlier was closing here in semiindifference and great weariness. No one any longer thought of speaking in praise of the tower; the tone is unambiguously "since it is there, let it stay." With a few exceptions, this was to be the line taken by all orthodox people of the twentieth century.

Not a Trace of Art

In 1890, Douanier Rousseau painted himself full length, with an air of great dignity, palette and brush in hand—*Myself, Portrait in a Landscape.* The background is Parisian: a metal bridge, high many-windowed apartment blocks, a forest of chimneys, and, behind them, aloft, slender, dynamic, apparently made of wood rather than metal, more a carpenter's masterpiece than the work of an engineer, the tower—the brand-new Eiffel Tower. The year before Seurat had painted it on a small panel before its completion. These are the incunabula of a long series of illustrations of the tower but also in some way the paradoxical conclusion of a lively debate which simultaneously involved painters and photographers, architects and engineers, and in which Eiffel's work played a decisive part.

Art or Industry?

Even today the endless discussion on Art and Industry is one of the most widespread—and before long the most tedious—ways of approaching the nineteenth century. Today, as yesterday, architect and engineer, or stone and iron, or Charles Garnier and Gustave Eiffel, according to the interest of the participants, meet in passionate exchanges. If one takes as a starting point these two prominent figures from the second half of the century, the desperate defender of stone and the man whom François Poncetton called the "iron wizard," one establishes connections between them that are both extensive and tenuous—extensive because they symbolize on the one hand the architect, and on the other the engineer; tenuous because the two men had only a few points of contact. The building of the Nice Observatory

(1885–87) and Garnier's presence on the commission for the 1889 Exhibition, at which his Histoire de l'Habitation Humaine was strung out at the foot of the tower, were the only two occasions on which they worked together, or at least on the same project. Nevertheless, it was the architect's statements in 1857 and the building of the engineer's masterpiece that opened and closed the long controversy on stone and iron buildings and their relationship with painting and photography.

For the issue was not only one of personalities, of priorities, or of commissions, not only a question of the suitability of a certain material to a certain building project, it was also a problem of representation and, in the strictest sense, of image. The progressive intrusion of engineers into what architects considered to be their exclusive domain did indeed set in motion the quarrel which raged fiercely during the Second Empire and at the beginning of the Third Republic and faded out—even if, as we have seen, many of the protagonists were entrenched in their positions—with the engineers' definitive victory represented by the building of the Eiffel Tower. This widespread, open controversy, endlessly rehearsed in the same terms right up to the present day, is mirrored in an equally bitter exchange on painting and photography, the merits and strengths of the one, the limitations and encroachments of the other. But the battles which iron and photography had to fight for their recognition are identical, since those who deny or belittle metal architecture are almost invariably those who deny or belittle photography.

In an article in *Musée des Sciences,* Charles Garnier sets out the issue explicitly and identifies its causes. He begins with a warning against the encroachments of all new inventions: "When any invention comes to reveal hitherto unknown materials and processes, it often happens that, through a desire to give them too wide a scope and to multiply their various applications, the limits which ought to be assigned to them are overstepped and a useful and advantageous system is replaced by one which is merely more or less ingenious." For the first time Garnier draws a parallel which is latent in all the subsequent debates: "In this way photography, otherwise destined to offer valuable service, comes every time to try to replace art with science, feeling with precision; in this way iron, whose use is greatly to be preferred to that of wood in almost all areas of construction, comes to encroach upon architecture, to change its characteristic forms and finally substitute industry for art."[1]

In the eyes of the future architect of the Paris Opera House, the regrettable results of this progressive invasion were already too clear to everyone, even if, to us, they seem limited and, in the end, hardly visible. He cited Louis Auguste Boileau's church of Saint Eugène, with its exposed metal structure, in which Garnier ironically sees the desire of the architect to "give an example of the bad effect produced by iron when it is used tastelessly and with the pretension of replacing stone, while more or less borrowing from it its rational forms."[2] This is the clearest possible position: iron is base, inescapably thin, and, when used on a large scale, it leads to the elimination of solids and visible points of support; it should be used with circumspection and systematically barred from every "artistic" construction. Kept to its proper function, metal is neither blameworthy nor without its uses, giving valuable service in all industrial building, railroad stations, exchanges, market halls, greenhouses, and so forth. The main thing is to define its role clearly and Garnier was preoccupied with this throughout his life. He railed at the multiplicity of the intrusions of iron and reiterated entrenched positions: "Iron is a means, it will never be an end."[3] He even issued a final and poignant appeal at the time of the preparations for the 1900 Universal Exhibition, when there was a threat of building a metal bridge on the extension of the Esplanade des Invalides (which was to become, though decorated and encrusted with cupids and garlands, the Alexander III bridge): "I beseech you, take up arms against scrap iron!"[4]

There was, at that time, another pariah, namely photography. How can one avoid comparing Garnier's remarks in 1857 with Baudelaire's famous passage on photography in the Salon of 1859? How can one fail to draw a parallel between the proclaimed "vulgarity" of iron and the "commonplace image" produced by photography? It was important to mark out carefully the bounds of this budding technique and Baudelaire painstakingly restricts the use of photography just as Garnier limits that of iron to utilitarian constructions. What photography should be is essentially documentary, "the very humble," though willing, "servant of the Sciences and Arts."[5]

To see the close link between the photographic eye and the metal object, one only has to look at the magnificent pictures which photographers have left us of the work of engineers, such as those published here of the Douro bridge, the Garabit viaduct, or the tower. For the engineer, photography is an opportune means of making himself known (for few people have gone to look at the structures built on the line from Commentry to Gannat); his works are shown to better advantage through photography than by any other means of representation, painting or engraving. It is enough to compare engravings made from photographs with the originals themselves to understand that photographs have a quite different effect in revealing the simplicity, lucidity of line, and functional purity of these constructions. Only photography can dramatize a work of engineering, emphasizing by a head-on, sharply angled, or oblique view the daring of the conception, the monumental nature of the object, the religious sense of awe that it inspires.

The limits set on iron, the restriction of photography's field of action—and their inevitable corollary, the strengthening of links between these two outcasts—was to some extent confirmed at a governmental level by the creation in 1866 of the twenty arrondissements of Paris, which had the avowed purpose of expelling industry to the outskirts of the city. Indeed, it was a question of protecting Paris from possible defacement through the large-scale presence of industry, just as some people wished to protect painting or stone buildings from the assaults of photography or iron. At the end of the fifties and the beginning of the sixties there was, then, a very strong desire on the part of some, if not a concerted effort, to create an "artistic" domain which would be free from the encroachments of industry. On one side Paris,

169 Douanier Rousseau, *Myself, Portrait in a Landscape*, 1890, Prague, Národni Gallery.

170 Georges Seurat, *The Eiffel Tower*, 1888, The Fine Arts Museum of San Francisco.

painting, and architecture in stone, on the other the suburb, photography, and the architecture of metal.

For a long time each side stayed entrenched in its position; photography was the impartial ally of metal architecture, while painting for the most part renounced it. Every encroachment gave rise to endless controversies. The most absurd rumors were spread. When, late in the nineties, the Compagnie d'Orléans wanted to establish a more convenient railroad terminus for travelers than the remote Gare d'Austerlitz, and secured a site left

vacant by the fire at the Cour des Comptes in 1871, many people feared not only the brutal intrusion of an industrial building on the Seine opposite the Tuileries, but also what seemed to them the inevitable consequences—the birth of a station neighborhood, the widening of access routes, and even the redevelopment of the Tuileries. Their fears were unwarranted; the imposing Gare d'Orsay has scarcely troubled the quiet of the Faubourg Saint-Germain.

In such a situation it is easy to understand what it meant to erect in the very heart of Paris a metal tower 300 meters high, which, moreover, would not disappear at the end of the Universal Exhibition. So the tower was symbolic in more respects than one. Certainly it was not the first metal construction in the capital; the numerous arcades, the greenhouses in the Jardin des Plantes, the metal-framed train sheds in the stations, Baltard's central market hall and the markets in the arrondissements bore ample witness to the presence of the engineers. In 1889, there was a clearly stated will to demonstrate this presence in a spectacular way.

Jules Simon was right when he penned a brief statement praising "this masterpiece of the builders' art," which was to appear in the popular, illustrated edition of the *Guide officiel de la Tour Eiffel:* the Tower "comes at its appointed hour, on the threshold of the twentieth century, to symbolize the age of iron which we are entering upon. From the second platform, and, above all, from the highest, a panorama unfolds such as has never been seen by human eyes. One may well contemplate here the march of the centuries. Nature and history are unrolled side by side in their most powerful guise. It is on this plain, stretched out beneath your feet, that the past comes to an end. It is here that the future will be fulfilled."[6]

With its "smokestack" shape,[7] the tower proudly reintroduced into Paris the industry which had been so carefully kept away. In raising this structure, which would "speak progress even to the heavens,"[8] the engineers, as Eugène-Melchior de Vogüé lucidly maintained, glorified the "victory of Science and Industry with a triumphal monument."[9] During one of his nocturnal visits, as he imagined a disquieting dialogue between the dwarfed towers of Notre-Dame, on which the searchlight had played for a moment, and their young metal sister, he attributed a proud and scornful speech to Eiffel's work: "Old, deserted towers, no one listens to you anymore. Don't you see that the earth's poles have changed and that it rotates round my iron axis? I represent the power of the universe disciplined by calculation. Human thought runs along my members. My brow is encircled with rays stolen from the sources of light. You were ignorance, I am knowledge."[10]

In the face of such "evidence," the famous Artists' Protest, signed by a number of "figures in the world of Literature and the Arts," gets bogged down in questionable arguments. Ridiculously worded, the epitome of sententious approxima-tions, this anthology piece still deserves to be quoted in its entirety:

Honored compatriot [the signatories are writing to Alphand], we, writers, painters, sculptors, architects, and passionate devotees of the hitherto untouched beauty of Paris, protest with all our strength, will all our indignation, in the name of slighted French taste, in the name of the threatened art and history of France, against the erection, right at the heart of our capital, of the useless and monstrous Eiffel Tower, which the caustic public, often endowed with good sense and judgment, has already dubbed the "Tower of Babel."

Without falling into an excess of chauvinism, we have the right to proclaim aloud that Paris is a city without rival in the world.

Above its streets, its broad boulevards, along its wonderful quays, from the midst of its magnificent promenades rise the noblest monuments conceived by human genius.

The soul of France, creator of masterpieces, stands resplendent within this majestic flowering of stone. Italy, Germany, Flanders, so justly proud of their artistic heritage, possess nothing which could be compared with ours, and from all corners of the universe Paris draws interest and admiration.

Are we then going to allow all this to be profaned? Is the city of Paris then going to associate herself any longer with the grotesque, mercenary inventions of a machine builder, so as to deface and deflower herself? For you must not doubt that the Eiffel Tower, unwanted even by commercial America, is the deflowering of Paris. Each one of us feels it, says it, and is profoundly grieved by it, and we represent only a faint echo of the universal opinion which is so justly alarmed. Finally, when foreigners come to see our exhibition, they will cry out in astonishment, "What! This is the atrocity which the French have created to give us an idea of their boasted taste!" And they will be right to laugh at us because the Paris of sublime Gothic, the Paris of Jean Goujon, Germain Pilon, Puget, Rude, Barye, etc. ... will have become the Paris of Monsieur Eiffel.

To bring our arguments home, imagine for a moment a giddy, ridiculous tower dominating Paris like a gigantic black smokestack, crushing

171   *Eiffel Tower Scarf*, 1889, Paris, Musée d'Orsay, Eiffel collection.

under its barbaric bulk Notre-Dame, the Sainte Chapelle, the Tour Saint-Jacques, the Louvre, the dome of the Invalides, the Arc de Triomphe; all our humiliated monuments, all our dwarfed buildings will disappear in this ghastly dream. And for twenty years, over the whole city which still trembles with the genius of so many centuries, we shall see stretching out like a blot of ink the hateful shadow of the hateful column of bolted sheet metal.

It is with you, sir, dear compatriot, who so dearly love Paris and have so greatly embellished her, who have so many times protected her against administrative devastations and the vandalism of industrial enterprises, it is with you that the honor rests to defend her once again. We entrust to you the care of pleading the cause of Paris, knowing that you will expend on it all the energy and eloquence which must be inspired in such an artist as yourself by the love of all that is beautiful, all that is great, and all that is right. And if our alarm call is unheeded, if your arguments go unheard, we shall at least, we and you, have given voice to a protest which does us honor.[11]

There followed the signatures of Meissonier, Gounod, Charles Garnier, Victorien Sardou, Gérôme, Bonnat, Bouguereau, Lenepveu, François Coppée, Leconte de Lisle, Daumet, Sully Prudhomme, Delaunay, Vaudremer, Dagnan-Bouveret, Antonin Mercié, Willette, Maupassant, and others.

The victory already achieved by the tower can be measured by the calmness of the response. In an answer to a journalist who had come to interview him,[12] Eiffel expressed his surprise that the protest had come so late—in February 1887, already two years after the plan had been submitted—and that Garnier, a member of the Tower Commission, had raised no objection: "He did nothing to show," Eiffel made clear, "that he did not approve of it, so he is protesting against himself." It was too late to do anything about it: the foundations were dug, the iron needed for the building was ordered.

When the reporter drew his attention to the fact that the protest was not aimed at building the tower but at keeping it after the exhibition had closed, Eiffel replied that in that case the protest was premature. No one yet knew exactly what the tower would be: "Up to now it has only been known by an elevation drawing; yet even though hundreds of thousands of copies have been made of it, is it possible to grasp the overall artistic effect of a monument from a simple drawing?" He then gently reflects on form: Is it because we are engineers that we do not pay attention to beauty? "Do not the laws of natural forces always conform to the secret laws of harmony? The first principle of the aesthetic of architecture is that the essential lines of a monument should be determined by their perfect appropriateness to their end. Now, what condition do I have to take into consideration above all others in a tower? Wind resistance. Well, I maintain that the curves of the four arrises of the monument, as the calculations have determined them, will give an impression of beauty because they will demonstrate to the viewer the boldness of the conception."

He went on to add another argument for the defense. The tower, standing on the outlying Champ de Mars, would not overwhelm the monuments of historic Paris. "Besides, the argument that insists that a high building must be overwhelming is one of the most invalid," and he quotes very appositely the example of the Opera: "See whether the Opera does not look more crushed by the houses in its neighborhood than vice versa." Thus he took up, to turn them against him, the arguments which Charles Garnier never stopped using to complain of the excessive height of the apartment blocks surrounding his masterpiece.

His final point, the tower's utility, was unanimously seconded by the scientific community. "Not only does the tower promise them interesting observations in astronomy, meteorology, and physics, not only will it enable Paris, in time of war, to be kept in constant contact with the rest of France, but it will at the same time be the dazzling proof of the progress made during this century by the engineer's art." Before mocking those among the signatories who were only known "for painting pretty little ladies dressing, or for having wittily turned a few couplets," before calling to the rescue the shrewd Vicomte de Vogüé who, in a recent article, reflected upon the vitality of "the spirit of France," Eiffel posed the question of prime importance: "Is it in no way for the glory of Paris that this summation of contemporary science should be erected within her walls?" There is no more pointed way of underlining the real grounds of the dispute.

Edouard Lockroy, the minister of commerce, forcefully supported the engineer; more unkindly than Eiffel, he noted "by the broad sweep of the periods, the beauty of the metaphors, the Atticism of the delicate and precise style [...] that the protest is attributable to the collaboration of the most famous writers and poets of our time," and, in saying so, rendered it ridiculous. He was, however, "deeply distressed" not for Notre-Dame, which would remain Notre-Dame, nor for the Arc de Triomphe, which would remain the Arc de Triomphe, but for "the only part of the great city that [is] seriously threatened, this incomparable square of sand which is called the Champ de Mars, so worthy of inspiring poets and capturing landscape artists."[13]

It was not only the signatories who were the great losers; many were in fact to make honorable amends, Gounod in particular writing some comic pieces "on the top." The major casualty was the particular concept of architecture doggedly maintained by Charles Garnier; ultimately it was stone masonry that appeared at the Universal Exhibition of 1889 as "played out, exhausted by its repeated use," no longer able "to lend itself to matchless innovations. It could only produce better disguised or more skillfully linked borrowings from old forms."[14] In short, it could no longer offer anything worthwhile.

So the tower compelled recognition, almost without striking a blow, as a "sort of anthology, summing up all the most widely held, current construction techniques."[15] In the Paris of 1887–89 it offered a completely new spectacle. The building site itself, as we have emphasized, had nothing in common with the other numerous building sites in Paris at that time. Whereas, in 1888, Léon-Paul Farge perceived "above the first platform a red halo of work, a sort of sonorous steam,"[16] it seemed to Vogüé, who almost never saw a workman on it, singularly calm and mathematical: "Few workmen were needed, and one was scarcely disturbed on the site because there was never a rasp from a file nor a blow from a chisel."[17] But when, as a privileged journalist, Emile Goudeau climbed up between the levels, the sight was quite different. "This platform"—the second; Goudeau was looking over the site at the beginning of 1889—"then looked like a brazier's camp. A thick smoke of coal and tar caught our throats and we were deafened by the sound of iron roaring under the hammer.

172   *Eiffel Tower Brooch*, Paris, Musée d'Orsay, Eiffel collection.

Over there they were still fixing bolts; workmen, perched on a seat a few centimeters wide, struck the bolts in rotation with their iron hammers. One would have said they were smiths quietly absorbed in striking rhythmical blows on the anvil in some village forge; only they were not hitting downwards, vertically, but horizontally and, as sparks flew out at each blow, these blackened men, magnified by the perspective of the open sky, looked as if they were reaping lightning in the clouds."[18]

On its completion the tower looked to the "fastidious," who did not like it, like a smokestack or a skeleton. Charles Garnier, always the dauber, pursued it relentlessly. "They have only put up the framework of this monument, taking care not to cover it with skin."[19] But above all it was baffling. Its "abstract, algebraic"[20] beauty was largely uncomprehended, which in no way injured its considerable success. Today nothing can better underline its astonishing modernity than Huysmans's harsh criticism of its "look of scaffolding,"[21] or its "broken-off posture."[22] This "triumph of brute fact,"[23] as François Coppée notes very precisely in an execrable poem devoted to the misdeeds of the tower, was, in the Paris of 1889, a big visual shock. One could leave Paris, like Maupassant, or carefully avoid it, like Verlaine, but to no avail, for it could be seen from everywhere.

The Tower as Icon

The novelty of the building operations, the strangeness of the building itself, immediately gave rise to an unprecedented iconographic flood, simultaneously popular and scholarly. On the site, photography played a considerable role; regularly used in this kind of reportage, it was not found wanting here. It was, besides, the only technique able to follow the exact and swift erection of the base of the tower and to show the steady growth of the pylon into the Parisian sky. In the great tradition of photographing works under construction—a tradition that goes back to 1850 and has Baldus as its greatest representative—Durandelle produced a magnificent album, *Travaux de construction de la Tour*, covering the work from the foundations in the barren Champ de Mars, the installation of the strong masonry foundations surmounted by metal shoes, up to its completion in 1889. The plates, showing from a distance the speed at which the giant puzzle was assembled, or, right inside it, the extraordinary network of trussed girders and wooden scaffolding, are apt to eradicate all human involvement. The tower rises mathematically, one might almost say by itself or by the force of circumstances; human intervention is reduced to almost nothing, an occasional head sticking out, if one looks carefully, between two iron girders. In this way Durandelle emphasized the formidable strength of the whole, a triumph of science and the engineer's skill rather than of mankind. We are closer to the algebraic vision of Vogüé than to the more colorful ones of most observers. Here there is no noise, not the least sound; under an unchangingly impassive sky the tower mounts silently and inexorably. Once again photography confirms the old alliance of the fifties by responding appropri-

173 *Eiffel Tower Bottle*, Paris, Musée d'Orsay, Eiffel collection.

178

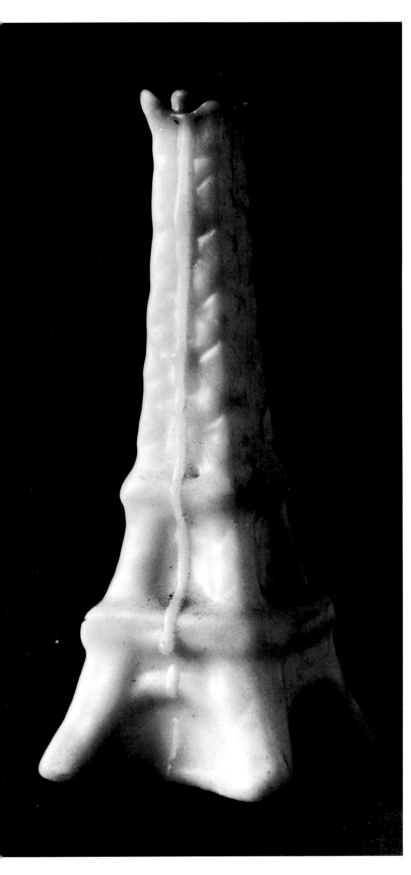

ately to the engineers' stated intentions: a "monument characteristic of pure science,"[24] "colossal iron pylon with the most fantastic spans."[25] It is the first to show the beauty of a work which refuses to make any concessions to decoration—setting aside those inevitably provided in the first-floor restaurants—and proudly presents itself in its new, skinless nudity: "Here there is nothing, no adornment, however modest, no flight of fancy, not a trace of art."[26] Only photography was equal to emphasizing this organic growth, which is incomprehensible to the passerby. "The tower progressively rose, one stage above another, as its sections, skillfully bound together, raised themselves ever higher. One saw the masterpiece, whose uprights seemed at first to take off at random into space, gather itself together, assume its relative proportions, in some way shrink into its strength and power, in order finally to present before the eyes of the wondering onlooker the immense nave of an unknown cathedral below, a spire of thrilling, unimagined daring above."[27]

For metal architecture and its chosen method of reproduction, photography, 1889 was—even if it was not always admitted—the year of complete victory, as assured, as mathematical as the elevation of the tower itself. It also saw the dissipation of the empty fears which arose at the end of the fifties—the assaults of iron were not so terrible, its results could be aesthetically pleasing—and along with them the collapse of all attempts at "reserved domains" which were being advocated at the time. The building of the Eiffel Tower and its photographic image mark the end of the thirty-year-old controversy. But immediately the problem arose of how to reproduce the inescapable motif which it had become in the Parisian landscape. For the formidable Huysmans there was no doubt: "Drawn or engraved, it is paltry."[28]

Like other major monuments, of which the Arc de Triomphe and the Statue of Liberty are nineteenth-century examples, the tower became the subject of an iconographic onslaught. From 1889, even before its opening, knickknacks, souvenirs, as well as poems and pieces of music proliferated: Eiffel Tower brooches, Eiffel Tower

174 *Eiffel Tower Candle*, Paris, Musée d'Orsay, Eiffel collection.

175 *Metal Model of the Eiffel Tower*, Paris, Musée d'Orsay, Eiffel collection.

176 C. Roüillar, *Two ▷ Clowns Juggling with Eiffel Towers*, 1887, watercolor, Paris, Musée d'Orsay, Eiffel collection.

182

◁ 177 A. Bourgarde, *'The 300-meter tower built up out of 300 lines,'* Paris, Musée d'Orsay, Eiffel collection.

178 *The Eiffel Tower under construction,* album of twenty-seven anonymous photographs, 1889, Paris, Musée d'Orsay, Eiffel collection.

goblets, Eiffel Tower candles. "During the construction, on the very site itself [...] M. Devic, one of the sightseers, seeing a bolt fall, had the idea of using the scrap from the tower [...]. On the spot he proposed that he should buy from M. Eiffel the unused material to make into souvenirs."[29] On November 22, 1887, an agreement was set up by which Eiffel undertook to release to Messrs Jaluzot

179   *View of the top of the tower,* album of twenty-seven anonymous photographs, 1889, Paris, Musée d'Orsay, Eiffel collection.

180   *The Eiffel Tower under construction,* album of twenty- ▷ seven anonymous photographs, 1889, Paris, Musée d'Orsay, Eiffel collection.

and Company, who for their part had agreed to accept them, "all the waste materials resulting from the building of the tower, at a price of 8 francs per 100 kilograms."[30] A little later the clever Jaluzot obtained the sole monopoly for three-dimensional reproductions of the tower for a period of ten years, which occasioned a commercial court case against Eiffel in the 1890s.

As well as these objects, there was an abundance of prints, photographs, and representations of all sorts. In 1889, Eiffel Tower waltzes and Eiffel Tower polkas could be heard, and even an Eiffel Tower symphony, the opus 63 of Adolphe David, a musician unacknowledged in any encyclopedia; a single movement—it might rather be called a symphonic poem—its sequences are linked

181   Henri Rivière, *The Eiffel Tower under construction in the snow*, plate from *Thirty six Views of the Eiffel Tower*, Paris, 1888–1902.

182   *The Eiffel Tower, Paper Model*, picture sheet from ▷ Epinal, 1889, Paris, Musée d'Orsay, Eiffel collection.

183   Henri Rivière, *Frontispiece from Trente-six vues de la ▷ Tour Eiffel*, Paris, 1888–1902.

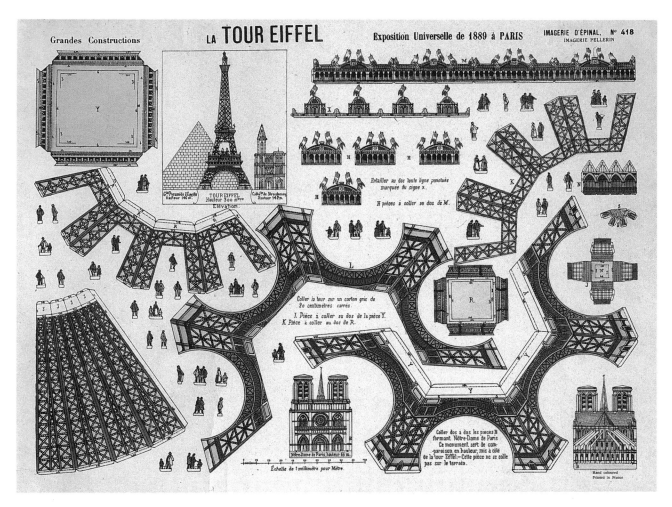

together like the accompaniment to a silent movie:

The arrival of the engineers and workmen at the Champ de Mars (lento)
Beginning of the tower's foundation works (moderato)
Sounds of iron (moderato e martellato)
The ironsmiths (allegro and cheerfully)
Tumult and trouble among the workers (allegro agitato)
First platform (andante cantabile)
Second stage, the tower mounts
Higher, the top (andante cantabile)
The crowd climbs up (moderato accelerando e crescendo al fine)
Hymn to the French flag (lento e grandioso)

The iconographic novelty of the tower was bound to give rise to new ways of modeling. Long ago Meyer Schapiro, the first of whose articles on this subject dates from 1935, emphasized the formal resemblance between the art of Seurat and the Eiffel Tower: "Besides, the construction of this immense monument out of small exposed parts, each designed for its place, and forming together out of the visible criss-cross and multiplicity of elements a single airy whole of striking simplicity and elegance of shape, was not unlike his own art with its summation of innumerable tiny units into a large clear form which retained the aspect of immaterial lightness evident in the smaller parts."[31] At any rate, for the first time, painting approached the construction head-on without picturesque asides and appropriated it without harm.

This extraordinary aptitude of the tower to arouse new modes of expression is shown even more clearly in two other spheres: calligrams* and photography.[32]

From the moment of its completion the tower gave rise to calligrams of which we still have several examples, dating from 1889, including a very curious one in Cyrillic script published in a Russian newspaper. It was as if the iron latticework was immediately suggestive of the construction of a poem, a homage in which the inevitable spaces in the writing correspond to the voids and solids of the metal tracery. But nowhere is this astonishing arrangement revealed as forcefully as in photography, particularly in certain snapshots taken by an unknown visitor in 1889, just as construction work was completed. Where Durandelle's album took its place in a recognized and long-standing tradition of photographs of works under construction, the unexpected meeting of the snapshot and the metal tower, the conjunction of these two innovations, produced images of a surprising modernity. The snapshot's small format, the enforced boldness of the viewpoints, the sections of the tower which they reveal in succession (where Durandelle saw it large-scale, from afar and as a whole), the almost constant human presence (where Durandelle saw it deserted), the smoke, the distances, the noise (where in Durandelle's there was nothing to be heard) produce a completely fresh vision.

Some of these views were retaken by Henri Rivière in his handsome album of *Trente-six vues de la Tour Eiffel.*[33] In what is a homage simultaneously to Hokusai and to the "immanent beauty of the great modern city of Paris," the tower is no more than "a good excuse," a "rod to hang the kakemonos on"; because henceforth one knew how to take it, as Arsène Alexandre rightly emphasized. Robert Delaunay was to prove it, and many others as well. This "total lack of sensitivity to art"[34] was already the whole of modern art.

---

* A visual representation made up of words—Trans.

184 Robert Delaunay, *Champ de Mars, Red Eiffel Tower*, 1888, 1911, Chicago, The Art Institute (Joseph Winterbotham Collection).

Last Works

The Panama Affair

It is the custom to close the account of Gustave Eiffel's engineering career with his masterpiece, the tower: having made his fortune, there was nothing to follow but the studious retirement of a scientific Maecenas, dividing his time between his luxurious house in the Rue Rabelais, the Château des Bruyères at Sèvres, and the estate of his son-in-law and collaborator Adolphe Salles at Beaulieu. The Panama affair, in which he was closely involved, though largely in spite of himself, had been the cause of this abrupt retirement from business. In his *Biographie*, anxious to supply the necessary explanation, Eiffel discusses it at length.[1] The Panama Company, which should have completed the sea-level canal by 1890, decided in view of the impossibility of carrying out this undertaking by the promised date to "substitute for it provisionally a canal with a series of reaches at different levels and large locks. This canal was to ensure navigation and full operation by the stipulated time and was to be gradually altered according to the original plan during the course of use." At the end of 1887, the hard-pressed company judiciously called upon Eiffel for this work, for he had, since Garabit and the commencement of work on the tower, been "known for the successful execution of particularly difficult projects." For the substantial sum of 125 million francs, the Eiffel Company was to construct at Panama ten locks, "whose grandiose scale was due above all to the unparalleled change of levels which they entailed. This change of level was indeed no less than 11 meters for seven of them and 8 meters for the three others. These works were carried out entirely to Monsieur Eiffel's plans, with completely new construction

methods, which inspired belief in their success. Opinion is unanimous that the realization of the scheme for the locks, which Monsieur Eiffel guaranteed on his own personal responsibility to complete in the very short span of thirty months from January 1, 1888, would have ensured the completion of the canal itself."[2]

The pavilion which he intended to build, at the end of 1888, for the Universal Exhibition shows the importance of this scheme, since a "model of the Panama locks," nearly 14 meters long, was exhibited there, sharing the limelight with the Garabit viaduct alone.[3] For Eiffel, the tower, Panama, and Garabit were manifestly his three most important works.

The problems were not new to Eiffel; in 1865 he had drafted a memorandum on his visit to the Suez Canal, and from 1886 onwards was thinking about "a canal from the Don to the Volga." Work had been under way for a year when the Panama Company had to suspend payments; shortly afterwards it was put into liquidation. For several months, in spite of everything, Eiffel continued the construction work; wanting to avoid the final collapse of the business, he advanced "more than eight million francs on very doubtful security."[4] In July 1889, however, the enterprise had to be brought to a conclusion and the accounts settled.

This protracted liquidation quickly became a scandal: after eight years of work and heavy financial outlay, how had things managed to reach that point? From 1892 the financial affair turned political; those "responsible" were tracked down and Eiffel was not spared. "And so he was wrongly implicated in the proceedings for breach of trust against de Lesseps, Senior and Junior, and other administrators; yet in this business he was nothing but a straightforward contractor acting in pursu-

GUSTAVE · EIFFEL
MDCCCXCI

185 Daniel Dupuis, *Gustave Eiffel*, 1891.

186 Salon of the Rue Rabelais house; in the background the portrait of Gustave Eiffel by Aimé-Morot (now in the Musée national of the Château of Versailles).

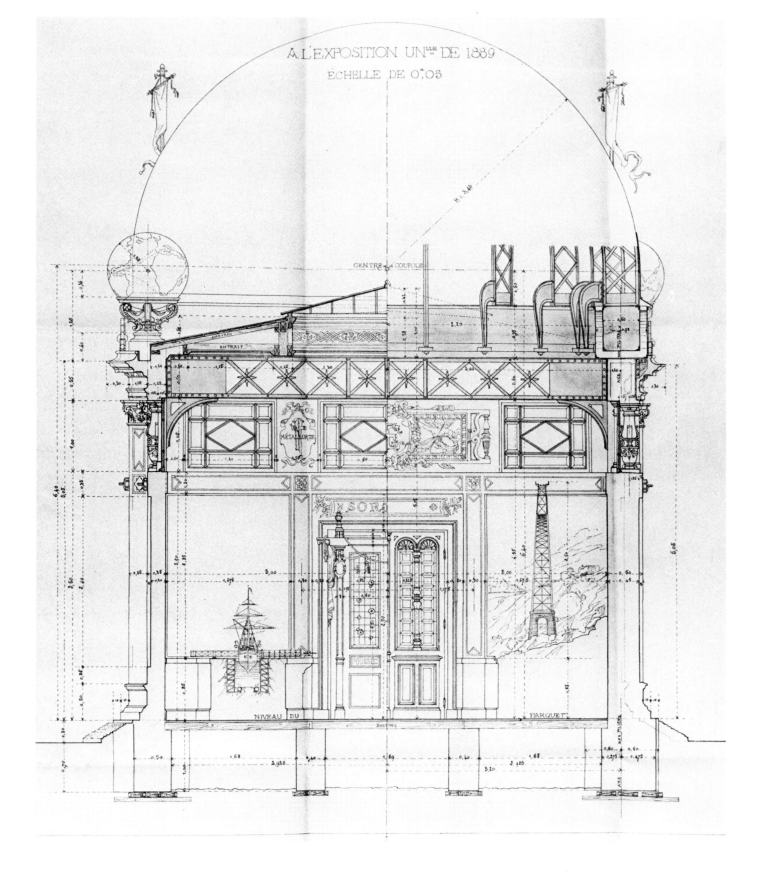

A L'EXPOSITION UNlle DE 1889
ECHELLE DE 0,05

187 Cassien-Bernard, *Plan for the Eiffel Pavilion at the 1889 Universal Exhibition*, cross section, 1888, print, Paris, Archives nationales.

188 Cassien-Bernard, *Plan for the Eiffel Pavilion at the 1889* ▷ *Universal Exhibition*, plans and elevation, 1888, print, Paris, Archives nationales.

PROJET DU PAVILLON G. EIFFEL
A L'EXPOSITION DE 1889.

ECHELLE DE 0,02   ELÉVATION   SUR L'ENTRÉE

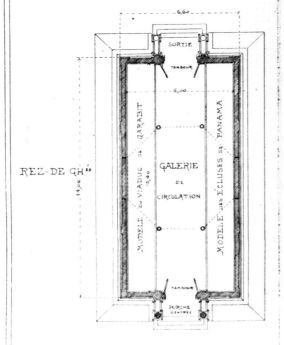

REZ-DE-CH^{ée}

PLANS

A

L'ECHELLE DE 0,01

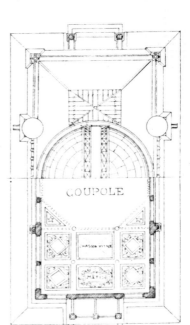

COMBLES

PLAFONDS

PARIS 18 XI 1888

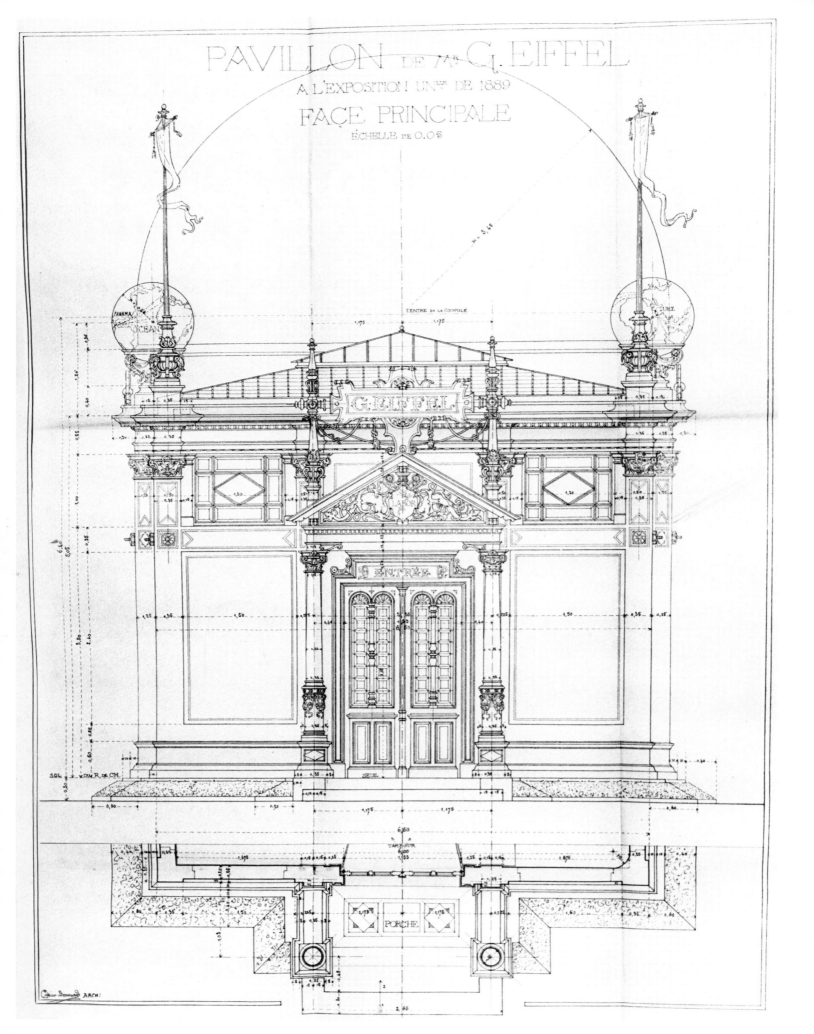

PAVILLON DE Mr G. EIFFEL

A L'EXPOSITION Unlle DE 1889
FACE PRINCIPALE
ÉCHELLE DE 0.05

ance of a limited contract, which released him from all responsibility in respect to the company's general transactions; and his accounts with the latter had reached a final settlement."[5]

In 1893, he was sentenced by the Parisian court but the judgment was quashed on appeal. The liquidators of the Panama Company had to pay Eiffel in full the amount still due to him. The engineer, "considering it a moral duty to help the

revival and reinstatement of the work as far as he could [...] took a considerable part, not less than ten million francs in the capital subscription of the new company, formed with the aim of completing the canal."[6]

The affair was not finished for all that. Following questioning in the Chamber of Deputies in December 1894, Eiffel, in his capacity as member of the Legion of Honor, was called before the Conseil de l'Ordre to give an account of his interest in the undertaking. After a long enquiry it was acknowledged that he was entirely blameless. But the harm had been done. Eiffel would never forget the affair; and he was greatly preoccupied by it on the very eve of his death.

The building of the canal slipped out of France's hands; the work begun by de Lesseps was taken up again by the United States in 1904 and only completed in 1914. An official American report, quoted by General Mangin in 1922, stressed the impor-

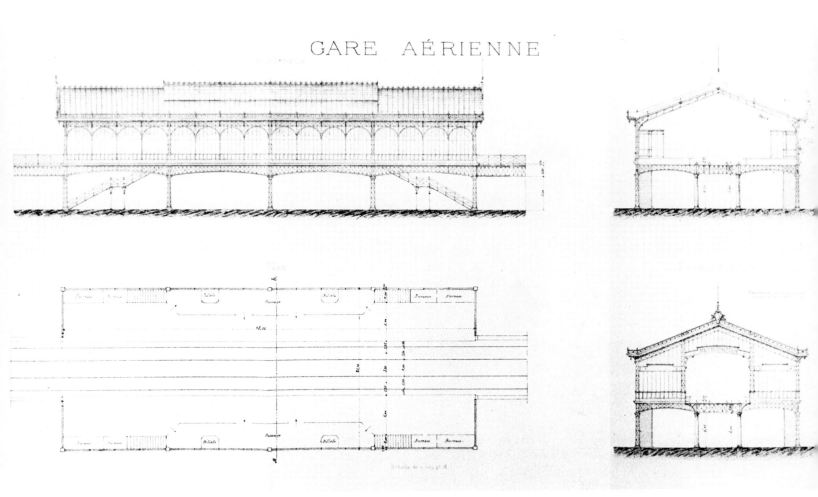

GARE AÉRIENNE

tance of the work which had been carried out beforehand: "Although the French engineers were not able to finish their task, their work at Panama was sound and of great value, *and in every respect they deserve the admiration of those who followed them.*"[7] Eiffel wrote out this last phrase in capitals; he was over ninety years old and for him it was a recognition, a justification, the proof of his talent and his probity in an affair which had wounded him deeply.

Abortive Projects

Between the time when Eiffel completed the tower in 1889 and his retirement in 1893 as chairman of the administrative board of the company he had

founded, he was occupied with three large-scale projects, none of which came to fruition: "the central metropolitan line in Paris," the "underwater bridge across the English Channel," and an observatory on Mont-Blanc.

On December 31, 1889, the limited company Gustave Eiffel and Company ceased to exist and

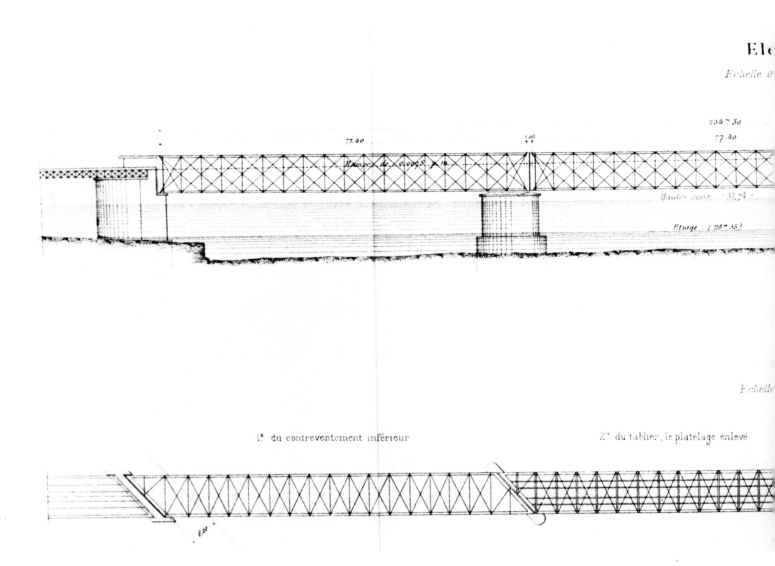

VOIE AÉRIENNE.
VIADUC MÉTALLIQUE.

Echelle de 0ᵐ02 p'mᵉ

Types Nᵒˢ 1&2.

Ensemble

Echelle de 0ᵐ01 p'mᵉ

Type Nᵒ1.

½ Coupe transversale
près d'une colonne

½ Coupe transversale
au milieu d'une travée

Type Nᵒ2.

½ Coupe transversale
au milieu d'une travée

½ Coupe transversale
près d'une colonne

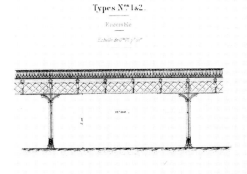

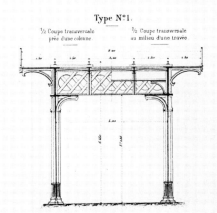

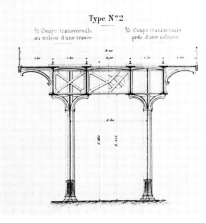

...tion.

par mètre

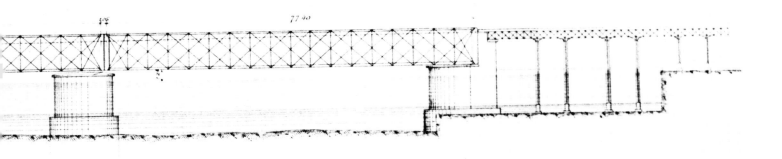

77 40

...ns.

02 par mètre.

3ᵒ du platelage et de la voie

GARE SOUTERRAINE

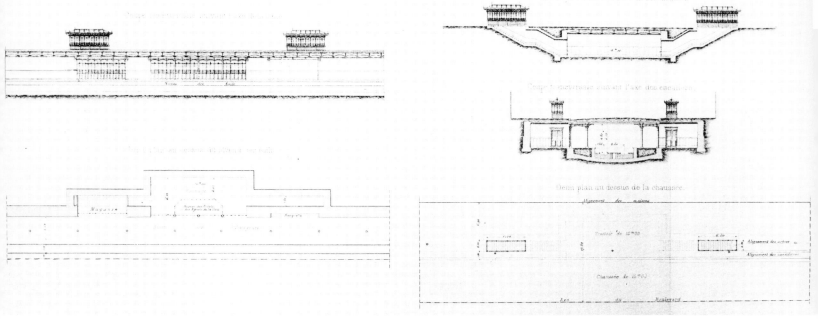

193   *Plan for the central metropolitan line, Paris, 1890, underground station,* longitudinal and cross section plans, print, Paris, Musée d'Orsay, Eiffel collection.

194   *Plan for the central metropolitan line, Paris, 1890, underground railroad,* variant cross sections, print, Paris, Musée d'Orsay, Eiffel collection.

VOIE SOUTERRAINE.

PROFILS - TYPES.

Echelle de 0ᵐ01 pᵐ

Profil . type Nº1 .

Profil . type Nº1 surbaissé .

Profil . type Nº2 .

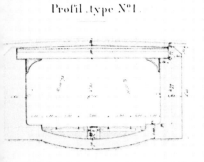
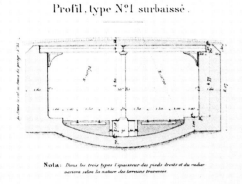
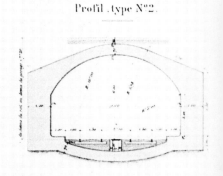

Nota: Dans les trois types l'épaisseur des pieds droits et du radier variera selon la nature des terrains traversés

was replaced as we have seen by the Compagnie des Etablissements Eiffel with a capital of six million francs. Eiffel was the majority shareholder and chairman, but he gradually handed over his interests before resigning three years later. The "strong man" of the business, since the building of the tower, when he had been able to prove his talent as an organizer and leader, was Adolphe Salles, Eiffel's son-in-law, who had married his eldest and, without question, favorite daughter, Claire. Once the tower had been completed, this brilliant Polytechnic graduate was put in personal charge of carrying out the construction work at Panama.

In 1890, when Eiffel proposed his "métro," it was in response to a promise already over twenty years old. The improvement of the Parisian transport system was a universally recognized need: London, New York, and Berlin were already well ahead in this field. "No question is worthier of the interest of the public authorities, for the improvement of the conditions of the largest and poorest class is intimately linked with its solution." So Eiffel sought a concession for "a railroad ring to be built in the center of Paris," a deliberately modest scheme, only 10 kilometers long; this modesty allowed him to do without public subventions and to be backed entirely by his own company "sup-

195 *"Observatory on Mont-Blanc,"* photograph, Paris, Musée d'Orsay, Eiffel collection.

ported by the major financial concerns in Paris."[8] Obviously nothing would prevent the subsequent grafting onto this central line of all the secondary networks it might be desirable to bring into operation.

The first plan for the Métro, dating from 1871, licensed the east-west cross line from the Bois de Boulogne to the Bastille. "The cross line from Boulogne to the Bastille had in its layout one section whose urgency was incontestable, the section included between the area of the Madeleine and the Bastille, and another much less important in terms of serving general traffic demands, that is to say, that from Boulogne to the Madeleine." For

Eiffel the western neighborhoods, recently built and inhabited by the middle class, did not demand the same concern as those of the center and the east, which were more working-class. He therefore substituted, for the Boulogne-Madeleine section, "a second east-west line following a route more or less parallel to the first; leaving the Place de la Concorde it would link up with the first line at the Bastille after having served the Gare d'Orléans and the Gare de Lyon, following the Rue de Rivoli and then the quais, from the Hôtel de Ville onwards."[9]

This layout, "really a flattened inner circle" like the one in London, had the merit of passing through the main-line stations, therefore making main-line connections, and of crossing the heart of the capital; so it would more easily link the business center and the inner suburbs, whose inhabitants often complained about the remoteness of the termini.

196 *Hut set up on Mont-Blanc*, longitudinal section, perspective view of the tunnel entrance, cross section, watercolor, Paris, Musée d'Orsay, Eiffel collection.

"The line is designed to be built in the open, on metal viaducts over a length of 2,555 meters, in walled cuttings or embankments over 100 meters, and in tunnels over 7,770."[10] Eiffel designed all the necessary permanent way and buildings, overhead stations (a design looking back to the covered bridge proposed in 1878), underground stations, tunnels, and light metal viaducts; but the project, which had many rivals, came to nothing. The first Parisian subway was only opened ten years later, after thirty years of procrastination.

Also in 1890 the Eiffel Company supplied drawings and calculations for an "underwater bridge to cross the English Channel." Consisting of a "watertight tube of cement blocks with a cast-iron envelope," the bridge—in reality a tunnel—was to be built "in such a way as to maintain its equilibrium in the water when not under load; in other words, in normal conditions its own weight would be equal to the buoyancy of the water."[11] Compared with the gigantic bridge projected by the Schneider Company, this scheme had the advantage of simplicity of construction, low cost, and minimal danger to navigation; it was nonetheless abandoned.

The idea of setting up an observatory on Mont-Blanc was due to a personal friend of Eiffel's, the astronomer Janssen who, from the time of the Second Empire, had made observations on Etna and in the Himalayas. A post on Mont-Blanc would facilitate those observations which "are the most subject to interference by artificial light and atmospheric absorption at lower positions, for example, the study of the planets Venus and Mercury, the telluric spectrum and the normal solar spectrum, and, finally, meteorological and physiological observations."[12] Drilling operations started in 1891; a wooden hut, built at Chamonix,

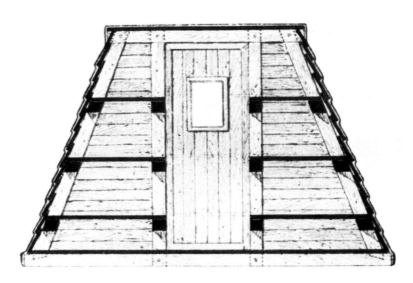

"demountable and easy to transport," was placed at the entrance to the gallery "in such a way as to prevent the blizzards from blocking it and at the same time to serve as a shelter for the workmen."[13] It was a difficult process: the huge quantity of snow, the force of the wind, the difficulty of communicating with the valley, and the death of a workman led Eiffel to abandon on September 4 an enterprise begun on August 13. Only 29.4 meters of the gallery had been dug—Janssen tried without success to revive the experiment. The only certainty which had been arrived at was the impossibility of putting up a building which could be "permanent, solid, and built under normal conditions." Perhaps the ice might have supported a light structure, for, inside the tunnel, it had shown itself to be "constantly homogeneous, with a fine texture, and, at its average temperature of –12 °C, extraordinarily cohesive and tough."[14]

Scientific Work

This failure affected Eiffel deeply; for a long time the problems of astronomy (which he had had occasion to study in Paris and then in Nice) had interested him; and those of meteorology even more so. The end of his life was entirely devoted to experiments in these fields and to the question of wind resistance. In his *Biographie*, he explains this progressive transition of his career as engineer and contractor into that of scientific Maecenas: "During the course of my career as engineer and on account of the exceptional scale of the construction works that filled it, wind was always an absorbing subject for me. It was an enemy against which I had to anticipate a constant battle, either during the building or afterwards. The knowledge of its force, which was deduced from that of its speed, therefore involved the study of the latter."[15] From the study of wind resistance he passed to the "consideration of other elements of meteorology," which necessitated the establishment of a fully equipped weather station on his property at Sèvres.

In 1889, Eiffel had installed an observation post on the tower; the following year at Sèvres he went on with a "French-type shelter," formed with a double roof, slightly inclined towards the south, and two small lateral shutters; then at Beaulieu in 1901, Vacquey near Bordeaux in 1902, and finally

197 *"Appareil de chute" for measuring air resistance*, view taken from the second platform of the Eiffel Tower before the drop (one of the sides has been removed), photogravure.

Ploumanach in 1906. Through the ten years from 1892 to 1901 he recorded at Sèvres a complete set of readings for air temperature, humidity, wind speed and direction, rain, mist, snow, and hail. He then extended his research over the whole of France, gathering together until 1912 the readings from twenty-five French weather stations.

From this date on the problems of wind resistance occupied all his attention. In 1910, he published a monumental work, *Wind Resistance, An Explanation of Formulae and Experiments*, "a work

198 *"Appareil de chute" for measuring air resistance*, the ▷ apparatus after the drop has been set in train in the stop cone (center, Gustave Eiffel), photogravure.

200 *Gustave Eiffel in the experiment chamber of his aerodynamic laboratory*, photogravure.

of compilation rather than an account of personal research,"[16] but one which for the first time presented a synthesis of "all work on this vast subject, whose importance, following the birth of aviation, was beginning to reveal itself."[17]

Eiffel's personal work in this field followed three stages: the installation from 1903 to 1905 of "appareils de chute"* on the Eiffel Tower, the experiments in the Champ de Mars laboratory

(1909–11), and finally those in the laboratory at Auteuil, which he established in 1912 and whose use he made over to the Aeronautical Technical Service in 1921.

In his *Biographie,* he clearly stated that "the problems which wind resistance poses, and which, thanks to aviation, have acquired considerable importance, have actually been encountered for a long time in several other branches of construction

---

* Apparatus for measuring the effect of air resistance on falling objects—Trans.

201 *André Granet's illumination of the Eiffel Tower for the 1937 Exhibition.*

work, notably that of large-scale metal structures exposed to the wind. In the designs for these, through lack of sufficient knowledge of the complex forces exerted by the wind, their builders were reduced to including in their calculations safety coefficients which had no scientific basis."[18] None of the great questions was answered—"Does the pressure increase or decrease with surface area? What is the pressure on oblique planes? Where is the center of pressure and how is it displaced?"[19] And this lack, in spite of the aleatory formulae which were available, complicated the builder's work.

The experiments made on the tower in 1903 provided the first data; in large measure they were undertaken to prove the utility of a building which was at that time threatened, as we have seen, with destruction. "They immediately determined the fundamental laws of wind resistance,"[20] verifying that wind pressure is closely proportional to the square of the speed.

A laboratory set up on the Champ de Mars from August 1909 to December 31, 1911, furnished with a suction fan driven by a 70-horsepower engine which was supplied with electricity by the post on the tower, made it possible to perfect the method of experimentation. The fan "drove into an airtight chamber a horizontal cylindrical column of air 1.50 meters in diameter and 3.60 meters long," which was directed onto the exposed surfaces "at speeds varying from 5 to 20 meters per second."[21] The resulting measurements verified the trials made on the tower for planes normal to the direction of the wind, squares, circles, rectangles of greater or less length, and certain three-dimensional forms such as cylinders, cones, etc."[22] Equally, the laboratory was the place where the first research was carried out on the "best profile for airplane wings,"[23] on complete model airplanes, and finally on propellers.

When he was obliged to give up his temporary shelter on the Champ de Mars, Eiffel took refuge at Auteuil where he "settled himself more spaciously."[24] Once more using the same type of wind tunnel, he increased the diameter of the air column to 2 meters and its speed to 30 meters per second (a little more than 100 kilometers per hour). When it was patented, the "Eiffel-style wind tunnel" was reproduced not only in France but in Holland, Japan, and the United States. The experiments on spheres were followed by "resistance trials on other rounded bodies," normal or oblique wire ties, tapered struts, airship hulls ... and also on airplane wings, and contributed to establishing "which were at that time the best of them."[25]

The war precipitated and defined more precisely the research, which now had a military significance, on the functioning of airplanes in flight, artillery missiles, and methods of releasing bombs.

Eiffel continued his experiments right up to the age of eighty-eight. In 1920, he withdrew from active life, but did not retire completely for all that, above all writing his invaluable *Biographie*, of which certain chapters had been drafted as long ago as the end of the previous century.

His end was gentle and happy: surrounded, respected, a "great man," proud of his work and his family. The conduct of his grandchildren during the war, especially that of his grandson, Georges Salles, the future Director of French Museums, had been heroic. He enjoyed a large fortune, was always full of curiosity and enterprise, on the watch for the most recent innovations, never senile or puffed up, a survivor from another age. He died, aged ninety-one, on December 27, 1923. Thanks to his grandson by marriage, André Granet (a great architect not nowadays appreciated), the tower, which was really a family business, was once again an attraction at the 1937 Exhibition, as up-to-date as it had been fifty years before, sending out showers of multicolored sparks from its platforms and lit up in red, white, and blue.

Appendices

Notes

Introduction

[1] J.M. Dufrénoy, *Album de Photographies: Dans l'intimité de personnages illustres, 1850–1900*, n.d.
[2] J.K. Huysmans, *Certains*, Paris, coll. 10/18, 1875, p. 405.
[3] G. Eiffel, *Biographie industrielle et scientifique*, preceded by a *Généalogie de la famille Eiffel*, 4 vols. in typescript, Paris, Musée d'Orsay, fonds Eiffel, ARO 1981–977 (a to d).

From Dijon to Levallois

[1] Eiffel, *Généalogie*, p. 17.
[2] Ibid., p. 4.
[3] Ibid., p. 11.
[4] Paris, Musée d'Orsay, Eiffel collection.
[5] Eiffel, *Généalogie*, p. 48.
[6] Ibid., pp. 49–50.
[7] Letter from Eiffel to his mother, February 21, 1860, Eiffel coll. ARO 1981 1144(a)8.
[8] Letter from Maître Chaffotte, Dijon attorney, to Madame de Grangent, February 10, 1860, Eiffel coll., ARO 1981 1147 (2).
[9] Letter from Eiffel to his mother, January 22, 1862, Eiffel coll., ARO 1981 1152 (5).
[10] Ibid.
[11] Eiffel, *Généalogie*, p. 52.
[12] Ibid.
[13] Ibid., pp. 54–56.
[14] Ibid., p. 57.
[15] Ibid., p. 63.
[16] Ibid., p. 64.
[17] Ibid., p. 89.
[18] Ibid., p. 90.
[19] Ibid., p. 65–66.
[20] Letter from Eiffel to his mother, January 28, 1860, Eiffel coll., ARO 1981 1144(a)1.
[21] Letter from Eiffel to his father, September 19 and 22, 1844, Eiffel coll., ARO 1981 1122 (3) and (4).
[22] Letter from Madame Eiffel to her mother-in-law, October 4, 1844, Eiffel coll., ARO 1981 1122 (7).
[23] Letter from Eiffel to his father, May 18, 1848, Eiffel coll., ARO 1981 1125 (4).
[24] Letter from Eiffel to his mother, October 12, 1850, Eiffel coll., ARO 1981 1129(a)3.
[25] Letter from Eiffel to his mother, January 30, 1852, Eiffel coll., ARO 1981 1133(a)1.
[26] Letter from Eiffel to his mother, May 23, 1853, Eiffel coll., ARO 1981 1135(a)6.
[27] Eiffel, *Généalogie*, p. 91.
[28] Ibid., p. 94.
[29] Letter from Eiffel to his mother, September 8, 1855, Eiffel coll., ARO 1981 1137(a)21.
[30] Letter from Eiffel to his mother, December 7, 1855, Eiffel coll., ARO 1981 1137(a)28.

[31] Eiffel, *Biographie industrielle et scientifique*, vol. 1, p. 3 bis.
[32] Ibid., p. 3.
[33] Ibid.
[34] Letter from Eiffel to his mother, February 13, 1856, Eiffel coll., ARO 1981 1139(a)6.
[35] Letter from Eiffel to his mother, May 30, 1856, Eiffel coll., ARO 1981 1139(a)18.
[36] Ibid.
[37] Letter from Eiffel to his mother, August 16, 1857, Eiffel coll., ARO 1981 1139(a)24.
[38] Letter from Eiffel to his mother, October 29, 1856, Eiffel coll., ARO 1981 1139(a)32.
[39] Letter from Eiffel to his mother, December 18, 1856, Eiffel coll., ARO 1981 1139(a)39.
[40] Ibid.
[41] Eiffel, *Biographie*, vol. 1, p. 4 bis; letter from Eiffel to his mother, March 29, 1858, Eiffel coll., ARO 1981 1141(a)13.
[42] Ibid.
[43] Ibid., p. 5.
[44] Letter from Eiffel to his father, December 29, 1858, Eiffel coll., ARO 1981 1141(b)2.
[45] Letter from Eiffel to his mother, December 9, 1859, Eiffel coll., ARO 1981 1142(a)6.
[46] Letters from Eiffel to his mother, July 18 and September 11, 1859, Eiffel coll., ARO 1981 1142(a)2 and 3.
[47] Letter from Eiffel to his father, March 17, 1860, Eiffel coll., ARO 1981 1144(b)1.
[48] Eiffel, *Biographie*, vol. 1, p. 5.
[49] Ibid.
[50] Letter from Eiffel to his mother, June 20, 1862, Eiffel coll., ARO 1981 1152 (22).
[51] Letter from Eiffel to his mother, March 15, 1861, Eiffel coll., ARO 1981 1151 (3).
[52] Eiffel, *Biographie*, p. 5 bis.
[53] Letter from Eiffel to his mother, October 15, 1862, Eiffel coll., ARO 1981 1152 (32).
[54] Ibid.
[55] Letter from Eiffel to his mother, May 22, 1863, Eiffel coll., ARO 1981 1153 (10).
[56] Letter from Eiffel to his mother, September 20, 1864, Eiffel coll., ARO 1981 1154 (26).
[57] Ibid.
[58] Eiffel, *Biographie*, vol. 1, p. 6.
[59] Ibid.
[60] Ibid., p. 7.
[61] Letter from Eiffel, December 4, 1886, Eiffel coll., ARO 1981 1156 (17).

The Bridge Builder

[1] On Levallois-Perret, see Pierre Hénon and Alain Thiébaut, *Levallois, histoire d'une banlieue*, Brussels, 1981.

[2] Emile de La Bedollière, *Histoire des environs du nouveau Paris*, Paris, n.d., p. 143.

[3] Contract concluded between G. Eiffel and T. Seyrig, Eiffel coll., ARO 1981 1414 (1).

[4] As regards the activity of Gustave Eiffel in the company he founded and of which he was managing director until 1893, the following files in the series 152 AQ in the National Archives are of particular relevance:

    106 Inventory and balance sheets 1889–92
    125 Plans of the installations at Paris and Levallois-Perret
    147 Bridge over the Douro
        Empalot bridge
    148–152 Garabit viaduct
    153 Tardes viaduct
    154 Universal Exhibition of 1889, Machines Gallery
    155 Bridge for Senegal
        Cubzac bridge
    156 Java railroad
        Nice Observatory
    157–158 Nice Observatory
    159 Nice Observatory
        Bridge over the Tagus
    160 Bridges for the local roads in the Vienne department
    228–232 Files on the portable bridges brought together as one document
    304 Douro bridge (drawings of details)
    305 Bridge over the Tagus (drawings of details)
    306–329 Garabit viaduct (drawings of details)
    330 Nice Observatory (drawings of details)

[5] François Poncetton, *Eiffel, le magicien du fer*, Paris, 1939.

[6] *Les grandes constructions métalliques, conférence faite par G. Eiffel, vice-président de la Société des Ingénieurs Civils à l'Association française pour l'avancement des Sciences, le 10 mars 1888*, Paris, 1888.

[7] *Nouveaux ponts portatifs économiques, système Eiffel [...] Notice sur les différents types des ponts de ce système*, Paris, 2nd ed., 1885, p. 5.

[8] Ibid., p. 7.

[9] Ibid., p. 55.

[10] Ibid., p. 56.

[11] Paris, National Archives, 152 AQ 231.

[12] Letter from Eiffel to his father, December 9, 1866, Eiffel coll., ARO 1981 1156 (18).

[13] Letter from Eiffel to his mother, December 30, 1866, Eiffel coll., ARO 1981 1156 (19).

[14] Letter from Eiffel to his father, February 22, 1869, Eiffel coll., ARO 1981 1158 (1).

[15] Letter from Eiffel to his father, March 22, 1869, Eiffel coll., ARO 1981 1159 (3).

[16] Letter from Eiffel to his mother, May 20, 1866, Eiffel coll., ARO 1981 1161 (6).

[17] Letter from Eiffel to his father, May 31, 1871, Eiffel coll., ARO 1981 1161 (8).

[18] Letter from Eiffel to his mother, May 20, 1866, Eiffel coll., ARO 1981 1161 (6).

[19] Letter from Eiffel to his mother, June 8, 1867, Eiffel coll., ARO 1981 1157 (11).

[20] Eiffel, *Biographie*, vol. 1, p. 8.

[21] Ibid., p. 9.

[22] Ibid., pp. 9–10.

[23] *Exposition Universelle de 1878, Notice sur les appareils, modèles et dessins exposés par MM. G. Eiffel et Cie, Ingénieurs-constructeurs à Levallois-Perret (Seine)*, Paris, 1878, p. 26.

[24] Letter from Eiffel to his mother, April 7, 1875, Eiffel coll., ARO 1981 1165 (8).

[25] Eiffel, *Biographie*, vol. 1, p. 25.

[26] *Exposition Universelle de 1878, Notice*, p. 28.

[27] Ibid., pp. 28–29.

[28] Ibid., p. 4.

[29] Théophile Seyrig, *Le Pont sur le Douro à Porto*, Paris, 1878.

[30] Paris, National Archives, 152 AQ 304.

[31] Gilbert Cordier, *A propos de l'œuvre de Gustave Eiffel*, Paris, n.d., p. 247.

[32] Seyrig, *Le Pont sur le Douro*.

[33] Ibid.

[34] Letter from Eiffel to his mother, May 17, 1875, Eiffel coll., ARO 1981 1165 (17).

[35] *Exposition Universelle de 1878, Notice*, p. 13.

[36] Ibid., p. 36.

[37] *Rapport sur le projet de M. Eiffel présenté par MM. Krantz, Molinos, de Dion, 30 juin 1875*, Paris, National Archives, 152 AQ 147.

[38] Douro bridge, *Mémoire présenté à l'appui du projet*, Paris, National Archives, 152 AQ 147.

[39] Ibid.

[40] Ibid.

[41] Ibid.

[42] Georges Barral, *Le Panthéon scientifique de la Tour Eiffel*, Paris, 1892.

[43] Eiffel, *Biographie*, vol. 1, p. 17.

[44] *Exposition Universelle de 1878, Notice*, p. 12.

[45] Seyrig, *Le Pont sur le Douro*.

[46] Eiffel, *Biographie*, vol. 1, p. 18.

[47] *Compagnies et Etablissement Eiffel (Entreprises générales et Constructions métalliques), Statuts*, Paris, 1890.

[48] *Rapport administratif sur l'Exposition Universelle de 1878, Paris, Rapport au président de la République, à l'appui du décret de 4 avril 1876, par Teisserence de Bort, ministre de l'Agriculture et du Commerce*, vol. 2, Paris, 1881, p. 8.

[49] "Exposition Universelle de 1878. Concours ouvert pour l'édification des bâtiments destinés à l'Exposition. Compte-rendu des projets primés, no. 60 projet de MM. G. Eiffel et Cie," *Encyclopédie d'Architecture*, September 1876.

[50] Ibid.

[51] Ibid.

[52] *Exposition Universelle de 1878, Notice*, p. 37.

[53] Ibid., p. 38.

[54] *Encyclopédie d'Architecture*, 1878, p. 83.

[55] Ibid., p. 32.

[56] *Exposition Universelle de 1878, Notice*, p. 38.

[57] Ibid., p. 39.

[58] *Les merveilles de l'Exposition Universelle de 1878*, Paris, 1878, pp. 106–107; cf. Henri Loyrette, "Des palais isolés à la ville dans la ville—Paris 1855–1900," in *Le livre des Expositions Universelles*, Paris, 1983, p. 227.

[59] *Exposition Universelle de 1878, Notice*, p. 39.

[60] *Exposition Universelle d'Anvers en 1885. Notice sur l'Exposition de M. G. Eiffel, ingénieur-constructeur à Levallois-Perret, près Paris*, n.p., n.d.

[61] Codicil to Eiffel's will, October 20, 1906, Eiffel coll., ARO 1981 996 (h).

[62] Eiffel, *Biographie*, vol. 1, p. 20.

[63] Ibid., p. 18.

[64] Ibid., p. 18.

[65] "Préfecture de la Lozère, décision ministérielle, 14 juin 1879," quoted in *Mémoire présenté à l'appui du projet définitif du viaduc de Garabit par M. G. Eiffel, extrait des Mémoires de la Société des Ingénieurs Civils, juillet 1888*, Paris, 1889, pp. 135–140.

[66] Barral, *Le Panthéon scientifique*, pp. 376–378.

[67] Ibid., p. 374.

[68] Ibid., p. 372.

[69] Paris, National Archives, 152 AQ 306 to 329.

[70] Paris, National Archives, 152 AQ 148.

[71] Eiffel, *Biographie*, vol. 1, p. 20.

[72] *Mémoire présenté à l'appui du projet définitif du viaduc de Garabit*, p. 180.

[73] Eiffel, *Biographie*, vol. 1, p. 14.

[74] Paris, National Archives, 152 AQ 153.

[75] Eiffel, *Biographie*, p. 15; *Les grandes constructions métalliques*, p. 15.

[76] Eiffel, *Biographie*, p. 26.

[77] *Les grandes constructions métalliques*, p. 13.

[78] Charles Talansier, *La Statue de la Liberté éclairant le monde*, Paris, taken from the journal *Le Génie Civil*, 1883, p. 10.

[79] Eiffel, *Biographie*, p. 27.

[80] Talansier, *La Statue de la Liberté*, p. 15.

[81] Ibid., p. 16.

[82] Eiffel, *Biographie*, p. 26.

[83] On the Nice Observatory, in addition to the valuable files preserved in the French National Archives, see the chapter devoted to this monument in Jean-François Pinchon's extensive *Catalogue de l'œuvre de Charles Garnier en dehors de l'Opéra de Paris*, Master's thesis, University of Paris-Nanterre, October 1981.

[84] Eiffel, *Biographie*, vol. 1, pp. 26–27.

The 300-Meter Tower

[1] Eiffel, *Biographie*, vol. 1, p. 44.

[2] Ibid.

[3] Alfred Picard, *Exposition Universelle de 1889 à Paris. Rapport Général*, vol. 2, Paris, 1891, p. 263.

[4] Vogüé, E.M. de, *Remarques sur l'Exposition du Centenaire*, Paris, 1889, p. 12.

[5] Ibid., p. 13.

[6] Picard, *Exposition Universelle*, p. 263.

[7] Ibid., p. 264; X… Engineer, "Tour de 300 mètres de hauteur," *Revue de l'Architecture et des Travaux Publics*, vol. XLII, 1885, p. 32.

[8] "Tour de 300 mètres," p. 32.

[9] Ibid., p. 34.

[10] Ibid.

[11] Picard, *Exposition Universelle*, p. 265.

[12] Ibid.

[13] Eiffel, *Biographie*, vol. 1, p. 44.

[14] Quoted by Bertrand Lemoine, *Gustave Eiffel*, Paris, 1984, p. 86.

[15] Ibid.

[16] Ibid., p. 88; G. Eiffel, *Biographie*, vol. 1, p. 45.

[17] *Tour en fer de 300 mètres de hauteur destinée à l'Exposition de 1889, projet présenté par M. G. Eiffel ingénieur-constructeur, dressé par MM. E. Nouguier et M. Koechlin ingénieurs de la maison Eiffel et par M. S. Sauvestre, architecte, Mémoire lu à la Société des Ingénieurs Civils par M. G. Eiffel*, Paris, 1885, pp. 5–6.

[18] Ibid., p. 8.

[19] Ibid., p. 17.

[20] Ibid., p. 9.

[21] Huysmans, *Certains*, p. 402.

[22] Ibid.

[23] *Tour en fer*, p. 23.

[24] Ibid., p. 30.

[25] Picard, *Exposition Universelle*, p. 265.

[26] Eiffel, *La Tour Eiffel vers 1900*, Paris, 1902, p. 9.

[27] Picard, *Exposition Universelle*, p. 265.

[28] Ibid., p. 280.

[29] "Convention relative à la Tour Eiffel," Eiffel coll.

[30] "Tour de 300 mètres—Résultat au point de vue financier," Eiffel coll., ARO 1981 1256 (1).

[31] Ibid.

[32] Note from Eiffel to the General Director of Works for the Exhibition, November 26, 1886, Eiffel coll., ARO 1981 1258.

[33] Max de Nansouty, *La Tour Eiffel de 300 mètres à l'Exposition Universelle de 1889, Historique et description*, Paris, n.d., p. 16.

[34] Ibid., p. 18.

[35] Picard, *Exposition Universelle*, pp. 282–284; "Notice du guide de la Tour Eiffel," typed copy corrected by Eiffel, Eiffel coll., ARO 1981, 1289 1 to 31.

[36] Picard, *Exposition Universelle*, p. 284.

[37] Vogüé, *Remarques sur l'Exposition*, p. 14.

[38] Picard, *Exposition Universelle*, p. 285.

[39] Ibid.

[40] Ibid., p. 287.

[41] Vogüé, *Remarques sur l'Exposition*, p. 14.

[42] Picard, *Exposition Universelle*, p. 287.

[43] Ibid., p. 289.

[44] Ibid.

[45] Vogüé, *Remarques sur l'Exposition*, p. 15.

[46] Ibid.

[47] Picard, *Exposition Universelle*, p. 290.

[48] Eiffel, *La Tour de 300 mètres*, 1 vol. of text, 1 vol. of plates, Paris, 1900, p. 100.

[49] Ibid.

[50] Ibid.

[51] Picard, *Exposition Universelle*, p. 291.

[52] Barral, *Le Panthéon scientifique*, p. 383.

[53] Picard, *Exposition Universelle*, p. 292.

[54] Ibid.

[55] Eiffel, *La Tour de 300 mètres*, p. 120.

[56] Ibid., p. 118.

[57] Ibid., p. 119.

[58] Ibid., p. 120.

[59] Picard, *Exposition Universelle*, p. 295.

[60] Ibid., p. 297.

[61] Ibid., p. 300; Gaston Tissandier, *La Tour Eiffel de 300 mètres*, Paris, 1889, p. 64.

[62] Picard, *Exposition Universelle*, p. 302.

[63] "Notice du guide de la Tour Eiffel," 1920, text quoted above.

[64] Eugène Reboul, *Souvenir de mon ascension à la Tour Eiffel*, Paris, 1889, p. 5.

[65] Emile Goudeau, "Ascension à la tour Eiffel," *Revue de l'Exposition Universelle de 1889*, vol. 1, Paris, 1889, p. 285.

[66] Reboul, *Souvenir de mon ascension*, p. 7.

[67] Ibid., p. 13.

[68] Goudeau, "Ascension à la tour Eiffel," p. 285.

[69] Ibid.

[70] Ibid., p. 286.

[71] Victor Navlet, *Vue de Paris prise d'un ballon*, 1855, Paris, Musée d'Orsay, Inv. 20 094.

[72] Vogüé, *Remarques sur l'Exposition*, p. 21.

[73] Ibid., p. 22.

[74] Ibid., pp. 22–23.

[75] Picard, *Exposition Universelle*, p. 314.

[76] Eiffel, *La Tour en 1900*, p. 43.

[77] Raymond Isay, *Panorama des Expositions Universelles*, Paris, 1937, p. 214.

[78] Texts collected in *Documents relatifs à la conservation de la Tour Eiffel*, Paris, December 1903.

[79] "Avis du comité-technique de la préfecture de la Seine (extrait du procès-verbal de la séance du 6 novembre 1903)," ibid.

[80] Ibid.

Not a Trace of Art

[1] Charles Garnier, "L'architecture en fer," *Le Musée des Sciences*, February 11, 1857, pp. 321–323.

[2] Ibid.

[3] Charles Garnier, *A travers les Arts, causeries et mélanges*, Paris, 1869, p. 75.

[4] Charles Garnier, "Letter to Bouvard on the 1900 Exhibition," Paris, Bibliothèque de l'Opéra, Garnier coll., item 18.

[5] Charles Baudelaire, "Le public moderne et la photographie," *Salon de 1850*, in *Œuvres complètes*, Seuil, 1968, pp. 394–396.

[6] *Guide officiel de la Tour Eiffel*, popular illustrated edition, Paris, 1897, pp. 5–6.

[7] J.K. Huysmans, *Certains*, p. 303.

[8] Raoul Bonnery, "La Tour Eiffel à François Coppée le jour de ses 300 mètres," *Le Franc-Journal*, May 1889.

[9] E.M. de Vogüé, "A travers l'Exposition," *Revue des Deux-Mondes*, July 1889.

[10] Vogüé, *Remarques sur l'Exposition*, pp. 24–25.

[11] "Artists against the Eiffel Tower," protest published in *Le Temps*, February 14, 1887; we refer to the manuscript in Eiffel's possession, which is followed by his reply, Eiffel coll., ARO 1981 1286 1 to 16.

[12] The quotations from the Musée d'Orsay manuscript show some alterations from the published text.

[13] Poncetton, *Eiffel*, pp. 168–169.

[14] Huysmans, *Certains*, p. 402.

[15] Roland Barthes, *La Tour Eiffel*, Paris, 1964, p. 63.

[16] Léon-Paul Farge, *D'Après Paris*, Paris, 1932, p. 35.

[17] Vogüé, *Remarques sur l'Exposition*, p. 15.

[18] Goudeau, "Ascension à la Tour," p. 282.

[19] Charles Garnier, "Le dîner de l'Ecole," *L'Architecture*, Year 5, No. 51, December 17, 1892, pp. 589–591.

[20] Vogüé, "A travers l'Exposition."

[21] Huysmans, *Certains*, p. 405.

[22] Ibid.

[23] François Coppée, "Sur la Tour Eiffel, deuxième plateau," quoted in *La Tour Eiffel*, with an introduction by Armand Lanoux, Paris, 1980, p. 56.

[24] Nansouty, *La Tour Eiffel*, p. 10.

[25] Ibid., p. 88.

[26] Huysmans, *Certains*, p. 409.

[27] Nansouty, *La Tour Eiffel*, p. 90.

[28] Huysmans, *Certains*, p. 406.

[29] *Tribunal de Commerce de la Seine, Mémoire pour M.G. Eiffel contre MM. J. Jaluzot et Cie*, Paris, 1891, p. 8.

[30] Ibid.

[31] Meyer Schapiro, "Seurat and La Grande Jatte," *Columbia Review*, November 1935, p. 15; "New Light on Seurat," *Art News*, April 1958, pp. 45–52.

[32] Eiffel coll., Pho 1981-124.

[33] Henri Rivière, *Les Trente-six vues de la Tour Eiffel*, prologue by Arsène Alexandre, Paris, 1888–1902.

[34] Huysmans, *Certains*, p. 405.

Last Works

[1] Eiffel, *Biographie*, vol. 1, p. 29.

[2] Ibid., p. 28.

[3] Paris, National Archives, 152 AQ 154.

[4] Eiffel, *Biographie*, vol. 1, p. 29.

[5] Ibid., p. 31.

[6] Ibid., p. 34.

[7] Ibid., p. 42.

[8] *Note sur la ligne métropolitaine centrale de Paris proposée par la Compagnie des Etablissements Eiffel*, Paris, 1890, pp. 3–6.

[9] Ibid., p. 9.

[10] Ibid., p. 12.

[11] "Calculations for an underwater bridge to cross the English Channel," manuscript note, 1890, Eiffel coll., ARO 1981 1409.

[12] Janssen, "Un observatoire au Mont-Blanc," paper delivered during the annual public meeting of the French Institute, Academy of Sciences on Monday, December 19, 1892, Paris, 1893, p. 16.

[13] Charles Durier, *Les travaux de M. Eiffel au Mont-Blanc*, Paris, 1892, p. 10.

[14] Ibid., p. 23.

[15] Eiffel, *Biographie*, vol. 3, p. 1.

[16] Ibid., vol. 2, p. 1.

[17] Ibid.

[18] Ibid., p. 3.

[19] Ibid.

[20] Ibid., p. 4.

[21] Ibid., p. 9.

[22] Ibid., p. 14.

[23] Ibid., p. 17.

[24] Ibid., p. 35.

[25] Ibid., p. 41.

Bibliography

Works by Gustave Eiffel

Account of the Douro Bridge, Porto. Paris, 1879.
Notes on the different types of Eiffel system portable bridges. Paris, 1885.
Account of the Garabit Viaduct. Paris, 1888.
Memorandum in support of the definitive Garabit viaduct project. 1889.
The 300-meter Tower. 2 vols. Paris, 1900.
Scientific work carried out on the Eiffel Tower. Paris, 1900.
The Eiffel Tower in 1900. Paris, 1902.
Ten years of meteorological observations at Sèvres (Seine-et-Oise) from 1892 to 1901. Paris, 1904.
Comparative study of meteorological stations at Beaulieu-sur-Mer (Alpes-Maritimes), Sèvres (Seine-et-Oise), and Vacquey (Gironde) for 1902. Paris, 1904.
Practical studies in meteorology and comparative records at Beaulieu, Sèvres, and Vacquey for 1903. Paris, 1905.
Comparative study of meteorological stations at Beaulieu, Sèvres, and Vacquey for 1904. Paris, 1905.
Current meteorological observations. Meteorological Society, 1905.
Analysis of "Practical studies in meteorology". Meteorological Society, 1906–.
General types of meteorological comparisons with reference to the study of stations at Beaulieu, Sèvres, and Vacquey for the first and second semesters of 1905. 2 vols. Paris, 1906.
Meteorological observations of the Washington Weather Bureau. Astronomical Society, 1906.
Temperature measurement in meteorology. Meteorological Society, 1906.
Climatological study of Beaulieu-sur-Mer during the period between December 1 and May 1, from 1902 to 1907. Paris, 1907.
Summary of the main work carried out during the war at the Eiffel Aerodynamic laboratory. 1915–18.
Study of the airplane propeller carried out at the Auteuil laboratory. Paris, 1920.
Meteorological Atlas for 1906, drawn from twenty-two meteorological stations in France. Paris, 1907.
Meteorological Atlas for 1907, drawn from twenty-four meteorological stations in France. Paris, 1908.
Meteorological Atlas for 1908, drawn from twenty-four meteorological stations in France. Paris, 1909.
Meteorological Atlas for 1909, drawn from twenty-five meteorological stations in France. Paris, 1910.
Meteorological Atlas for 1910, drawn from twenty-five meteorological stations in France. Paris, 1911.
Meteorological Atlas for 1911, drawn from twenty-five meteorological stations in France. Paris, 1912.
Meteorological Atlas for 1912, drawn from twenty-five meteorological stations in France. Paris, 1913.
Experimental research on wind resistance undertaken on the Eiffel Tower. Paris, 1907.
Wind resistance: An examination of formulae and experiments. Paris, 1910.
Wind resistance and aviation. Experiments carried out at the Champ de Mars laboratory. Paris, 1910.
Wind resistance and aviation. Experiments carried out at the Champ de Mars laboratory. 2nd ed. Paris, 1911.
New research into wind resistance and aviation, carried out at the Auteuil laboratory. Paris, 1914.

Selected Bibliography

Barral, G. *The Scientific Pantheon of the Eiffel Tower.* Paris, 1892.
Barthes, R. *The Eiffel Tower.* Paris, 1964.
Besset, M. *Gustave Eiffel.* Paris, 1957.
Braibant, Ch. *History of the Eiffel Tower.* Paris, 1964.
Conte, A. *Tower Photograph Album Explained by Arthur Conte.* Paris, 1980.
Cordat, Ch. *The Eiffel Tower.* Preface by Le Corbusier. Paris, 1955.
Cordier, G. *About Gustave Eiffel's Work. Documents and Reflections Relating to the Circumstances and Construction Methods of the Nineteenth Century.* Paris, 1978.
Durier, Ch. *M. Eiffel's Work on Mont-Blanc.* Paris, 1892.
Guy, G. *A Tower Named Eiffel.* Paris, 1957.
Harris, J. *The Tallest Tower; Eiffel and the "Belle Epoque".* Boston, 1975.
Isay, J. *Panorama of the Universal Exhibitions.* Paris, 1937.
Landon, F. *The Eiffel Tower, Superstar.* Paris, 1979.
Lanoux, A. *The Eiffel Tower Introduced by Armand Lanoux.* Paris, 1980.
Lemoine, B. *Gustave Eiffel.* Paris, 1984.
Loyrette, H. "Photographers and Engineers." *Photographies,* No. 5, July 1984, pp. 12–18.
Marrey, B. *Gustave Eiffel and His Times.* Exhibition catalogue from the Musée de la Poste. Paris, 1983.
—*The Life and the Outstanding Work of Gustave Eiffel.* Paris, 1984.
Nansouty, M. de *The 300-meter Tower Built on the Champ de Mars.* Paris, n.d.
Poncetton, F. *Gustave Eiffel, the Iron Wizard.* Paris, 1939.
Picard, A. *International Universal Exhibition in Paris, 1889. General Report.* Paris, 1891.
Prévost, J. *Eiffel.* Paris, 1929.
Talansier, Ch. *The Statue of Liberty Lighting the World.* Paris, 1883.
Tissandier, A. *The 300-meter Eiffel Tower.* Paris, 1889.
Trachtenberg, M. *The Statue of Liberty.* London, 1976.
The Universal Exhibitions Book, 1851–1989. Paris, 1983.
Vogüé, E.M. de *Comments on the Centennial Exhibition.* Paris, 1889.

Index

Sources

The major collection of biographical documents relating to Gustave Eiffel and his family is housed in the Musée d'Orsay (Eiffel collection). The Eiffel collection, generously donated in 1981 by Mademoiselle Solange Granet, Madame Bernard Granet and her children, the engineer's descendants, comprises an important collection of letters (essential for Gustave Eiffel's beginnings), the four typescript volumes of the *Biographie industrielle et scientifique*, preceded by a *Généalogie de la famille Eiffel*, family photographs as well as photographs of his major works (notably an exceptional series on the construction of the tower), portraits, family souvenirs, Eiffel Tower mementos, and so on.

The archives of the successive companies which have occupied the Eiffel workshops at Levallois-Perret have been divided between the Société Nouvelle d'Exploitation de la Tour Eiffel (S.N.T.E.), which holds the documents concerned with the tower, and the National Archives, which has those relating to other constructions. References for the documents used are given in the notes.

Photo Credits

The author and the publishers wish to thank all those who have supplied photographs for this book. The numbers refer to the plates. The photo research for this book was done by Ingrid de Kalbermatten.

The Art Institute of Chicago 184
Bulloz, Paris 109, 152
Jean-Loup Charmet, Paris 1, 2, 3, 4, 5, 7, 9, 18, 19, 21, 22, 23, 24, 25, 26, 27, 28, 29, 30, 33, 34, 35, 36, 38, 39, 40, 41, 42, 43, 44, 45, 46, 47, 48, 49, 54, 55, 56, 57, 58, 59, 60, 61, 62, 63, 64, 65, 66, 67, 68, 69, 70, 71, 72, 73, 74, 75, 81, 82, 83, 84, 85, 86, 87, 88, 92, 99, 105, 111, 144, 145, 146, 147, 148, 149, 150, 153, 156, 157, 164, 166, 182, 186, 187, 188, 189, 190, 191, 192, 193, 194, 195, 197, 198, 199, 200

Eidgenössische Technische Hochschule, Zurich 106
The Fine Arts Museum of San Francisco 170
Národni Galerie, Prague 169
Réunion des Musées Nationaux, Paris 6, 8, 10, 11, 12, 13, 14, 15, 16, 17, 31, 32, 50, 51, 52, 53, 76, 77, 78, 79, 80, 89, 93, 94, 95, 100, 103, 104, 107, 108, 110, 112, 113, 114, 115, 116, 118, 120, 121, 122, 123, 124, 125, 126, 127, 128, 129, 130, 131, 132, 133, 134, 135, 136, 137, 138, 139, 140, 141, 142, 143, 154, 159, 160, 162, 163, 167, 168, 171, 172, 173, 174, 175, 176, 178, 179, 180, 185

Author's archives: 20, 37, 90, 91, 96, 97, 98, 101, 102, 117, 119, 151, 155, 158, 161, 165, 177, 181, 183, 201

Setting: Febel AG, Basle
Printing: Bund-Druck AG, Berne
Binding: Burkhardt AG, Mönchaltorf-Zurich
Photolithographs (color): Steiner + Co. AG, Basle
(black and white): Atesa-Argraf SA, Geneva and Schwitter AG, Basle
Design and production: Franz Stadelmann

Printed in Switzerland